Acclaim for Rafe Esquith and

THERE ARE NO SHORTCUTS

"Politicians, burbling over how to educate the under-class, would do well to stop by Rafe Esquith's fifth-grade class as it mounts its annual Shakespeare play. Sound like a grind? Listen to the peals of laughter bouncing off the classroom walls." —*Time*

"Rafe Esquith is my only hero."
—Sir Ian McKellen

"For ten hours each day, Esquith and his fifth-graders are holed up in their cramped classroom, immersed in a world of Shakespearean plays and algebraic equations, of classical music and fine lit-erature—a far cry from the gritty world outside the schoolyard's chain-link fence."
—*Los Angeles Times*

"What this group of students and their remarkable teacher are proving is that kids with no secure homes and no secure future can learn to hope and to become first-class citizens. If there's anything more important than that, please tell me what it is."
—Hal Holbrook

"Passionate and inspiring. . . . With anecdotes that are alternately amusing and disheartening, Esquith details the joys and frustrations of teaching and offers valuable insights to parents and teachers alike."　　　　　　　　　　　　　　　*—Booklist*

"Any teacher, parent or reader who cares about education in this country and who takes the time to read and synthesize Esquith's ideas will be rewarded."　　　　　　　　　*—Anniston Star*

"Upbeat [and] witty. . . . Part memoir, part manual, but primarily a call for action."
　　　　　　　　　　　　　　—Publishers Weekly

RAFE ESQUITH

THERE ARE NO SHORTCUTS

Rafe Esquith has taught at Hobart Elementary School in Los Angeles for nineteen years. He is the product of the Los Angeles public schools and a graduate of UCLA. His many honors and awards include a National Medal of the Arts, the 1992 Disney National Outstanding Teacher of the Year Award, a Sigma Beta Delta Fellowship from Johns Hopkins University, *Parents* magazine's As You Grow Award, Oprah Winfrey's Use Your Life Award, and an MBE from Queen Elizabeth. He lives in Los Angeles with his wife, Barbara Tong.

THERE ARE NO SHORTCUTS

RAFE ESQUITH

Anchor Books
A Division of Random House, Inc.
New York

FIRST ANCHOR BOOKS EDITION, MAY 2004

Copyright © 2003 by Rafe Esquith

All rights reserved under International and Pan-American Copyright Conventions. Published in the United States by Anchor Books, a division of Random House, Inc., New York, and simultaneously in Canada by Random House of Canada Limited, Toronto. Originally published in hardcover in the United States by Pantheon Books, a division of Random House, Inc., New York, in 2003.

Anchor Books and colophon are trademarks of Random House, Inc.

Permissions acknowledgments appear on page 211.

The Library of Congress has cataloged the Pantheon edition as follows:
Esquith, Rafe.
There are no shortcuts / Rafe Esquith.
p. cm.
1. Esquith, Rafe. 2. Teachers—California—Los Angeles—Biography.
3. Motivation in education. I. Title.
LA2317.E78 A3 2003
372.11'0092—dc21   2002075961

Anchor ISBN: 1-4000-3083-8

Author photograph © Peter Thomas/Dunlap-Turney Studio
Book design by Iris Weinstein

www.anchorbooks.com

Printed in the United States of America
20 19 18 17 16 15 14 13 12

For my parents,
Joseph and Claire,
who never saw me teach,

And Barbara.

CONTENTS

The Boxer

In the clearing stands a boxer
And a fighter by his trade—
And he carries the reminders
Of every glove that laid him down
Or cut him till he cried out,
In his anger and his shame:
"I am leaving I am leaving"
But the fighter still remains.

— PAUL SIMON

My father was a boxer. He fought almost a hundred amateur bouts and two professional ones. My mother made him quit the ring, but he was always a boxer. In 1948 he was called before the House Un-American Activities Committee. They couldn't knock him down—he told them nothing, and they never laid a glove on him; he always answered the bell. Even on his deathbed, heavily medicated to kill the pain from cancer, the forty-eight-year-old social worker kept asking his nurses, "May I help you?"

My mother raised me to help others. That's why I teach.

We teachers are all boxers. We get hit a lot. I've been knocked down so many times I'm often woozy.

But I've learned something in my first nineteen years in the classroom: all teachers, even the best ones, get knocked down. The difference between the best ones and the others is that the best ones always get up to answer the bell.

May you always get up. It is a child ringing the bell, and he needs your help.

THERE ARE NO SHORTCUTS

CHAPTER I

Curtains

It's dangerous to think too much about public education. So many things are wrong with it that it's easier simply to go on a search-and-destroy mission and write only about the horror of it all. Those of us who have survived school have plenty of scars. Any person who has taught for more than a few years has met administrators, teachers, parents, and children who, as Mark Twain once remarked, "make a body ashamed of the human race."

That's not my mission here. More than anything else, this book is meant to be a reminder of what public education can be. But to understand where we might consider going, it becomes painfully necessary to examine some things that we usually try to avoid.

I have one more objective, too: I want to give hope to young teachers who would like to run against the wind but are afraid of the consequences. I am living proof that you can have success as a teacher despite the many forces that are working against you. Like the Founding Fathers, I am a lover of independence, and freethinkers are not popular in public schools today. Instead, as public schools fail, bureaucrats are attempting to solve serious problems with simplistic solutions. They're afraid to examine the real reasons why our schools are failing, so they use fashionable words or pretty new textbooks to try and solve the very real problems that are destroying our classrooms. Poverty, greed, and incompetent teaching are just some of the reasons why Johnny not only can't read but has no interest in reading. Using a new reading series or changing the classroom environment isn't going to solve our problems. Most tragic of all, many districts are trying to take charge of education by forcing all teachers to use uniform lesson plans, by which all students will be guided in the same way at the same pace. This may be a comfort to young teachers who aren't sure what to do every day, but I already know the inevitable result of uniform teaching: things will continue to be uniformly terrible.

I've never been one of the masses, either as a parent or as a teacher. I will not let advertisers persuade me to see mediocre movies, and I do not watch a television show in order to converse with peers about it the following day. My life is my own. I don't feel I have to buy in to the popular culture in order to be a successful teacher, parent, or person. But there are those to whom fitting in with the majority is important, and I have respect for that path; it's just not the one I can follow, and these people may find the lessons I've learned irrelevant for their journey.

However, if you're a young teacher or parent who has

often wanted to break from the pack but has been afraid to do so, I can tell you that I've done so and am still standing. I have many scars and bruises, but I have, as Robert Frost tells us, taken the road less traveled. And it's made all the difference.

Most teachers who are honest look back on their first years in the classroom through half-closed eyes. Teaching is a tough job at any time, and I've yet to meet anyone who excelled at it from the start. It takes years of experience to develop the wisdom that can lead to being a first-rate teacher.

I was definitely a slow learner, and I had an interesting but painful experience when I was student-teaching in UCLA's Graduate School of Education program. I thought I was doing a pretty good job and was vigorously supported by the master teacher who supervised my work in her sixth-grade classroom. She particularly liked the reading program I designed for the students, most of whom spoke Spanish as their primary language. Rather than using the boring school reader assigned by the school district, I'd been reading the classics with these kids, and their reading and enthusiasm for literature increased enormously. For our final project of the year, we read *Romeo and Juliet.* My plan was to take the kids to the Franco Zeffirelli film on a weekend. It was playing in a revival house that showed classic films (this was before video made the showing of movies in class much easier).

The children got very excited about this trip and read *Romeo and Juliet* with gusto. They were devastated on the Friday we finished when our principal sent me a note telling me he had heard about my plan but that it was strictly forbidden to take students out on a Saturday. He went on to threaten that if the trip went ahead as planned, I would not receive a positive evaluation at the end of my student-teaching assignment.

I was furious and just crumpled up his note. I had worked for two months to get the kids ready for this trip. Their parents were supportive, and many of them were coming to the movie with their children. I couldn't believe the head of a school would want to prevent his kids from having a rewarding climax to their experience with Shakespeare. Looking back, I laugh at myself that a decision like that surprised me. I was so young.

I stormed into the office, gave the crumpled note to the principal's secretary, and told her to tell him where he could stick it. That afternoon, when I arrived at UCLA for my education classes, I was informed by one of the instructors that I had been suspended until a committee could decide if I had the moral character to be a good teacher. The fact that the movie trip was canceled was the least of my problems.

I went home too angry to cry, and terrified at the thought of never teaching again. I had spent much of my life planning to be a teacher and now I had to consider the possibility that because of this stupid incident I might have to do something truly awful, like go to law school. This frustration was exacerbated when I received my first lesson in educational hypocrisy. There were rumors that the principal who was angry with me was having an affair with one of the teachers (they were both married), and that she was pregnant. Now, I'm no saint, but it was hard to have my moral integrity judged by this hypocrite.

To make a long story short, they allowed me to go on being a teacher if I completely discounted the last six months of student teaching and repeated them. To punish me, they had me supervised by a struggling new teacher who had often come to me for assistance when we were attending class together the previous year. Despite her self-acknowledged shortcomings as a classroom leader, she graduated on time and got a job immediately. Well, I give them credit: if their goal was to humble me and teach me my place, they did so. I learned quickly that I was in no position to talk back to principals.

I wanted to be a teacher so desperately that I swallowed my pride, said all the right things, and received my teaching credential the following year. I was so glad to survive this ordeal that I didn't take the time to consider the lesson I should have been learning. I still mistakenly believed that this incident was an unusual one, and that when I was actually teaching and being paid for it, I'd be supervised by caring and able people who had dedicated their lives to the betterment of young human beings. I didn't realize that many people, who may be good people, feel that working in schools is just a job and not a holy mission. Instead, I was more interested in the fact that within the next two years, the principal who had written me the note went through a divorce; his wife had never forgiven him when his illegitimate child was born. Sadly, a year later he was diagnosed with cancer and died soon after.

I had missed a crucial lesson here, but I would be given countless opportunities in the future to learn it. Public education is a mess, and I had survived my first scare by allowing the powers that be to force me to do exactly what they wanted.

This is a natural danger for many young teachers. In truth, for many of us the initial objective is just to survive; we hope our lessons go smoothly and the clock runs quickly. For many novice teachers, there is no more wonderful sound than the dismissal bell signaling the end of the day. Consequently, in far too many classrooms the children's education is not the main objective. Older teachers often mentor the young ones by teaching them survival tips that are fine for the beginning teacher but not helpful to the student. As a result, many young teachers believe they're doing a good job when in fact they're using smoke and mirrors. They have beautifully decorated classrooms with all the school standards created by some bureaucrat hanging on the wall. Their kids walk in straight lines, and order carries the day.

It is painful to reflect on this, because that was my classroom for the first couple of years, and I, too, thought I was doing a good job. What's more, the kids liked me. God, how foolish I feel now, remembering those desperate days. I actually worried more about the kids liking me than if they were reading well.

But I was fortunate. I had planned to teach at a school in an economically disadvantaged neighborhood. Instead, I was assigned to a middle-class school with middle-class parents and middle-class values. There were only three hundred children at this school, and everybody spoke English. The kids had private music lessons at home. Everyone was on a soccer team or in a drama club or in an orchestra on Saturdays. They went to school liking their teachers before they had met them. I used to joke with my friends and tell them that I taught at a school called Camelot. I felt wonderful, until one day, by accident, a very nice little girl said something to me that started me down a different path.

Our school was having a fund-raiser, and every teacher was supposed to contribute something for a silent auction. One teacher contributed tennis lessons; another was taking four kids to the movies. Since I loved Shakespeare, I planned a trip to the Old Globe Theater in San Diego for a group of about twenty-five students. The plan was for some parents, teachers, and me to drive the kids down for a weekend and two plays. The parents would pay for the trip and add about $25 extra. In this way the trip made a profit for the school while the kids had a good time and learned something.

And they did indeed. The trip ran like clockwork. We stayed at a beautiful hotel with a Hawaiian atmosphere. The kids swam in an Olympic-size pool in the afternoons and returned to their lovely and spacious rooms to change before dinner. We saw two terrific plays: *Rashomon* and a particularly hilarious *Merry Wives of Windsor*. A splendid time was had by all.

It was Sunday afternoon and we were heading to the cars for our return to Los Angeles. Walking next to a perky little girl named Jenny, I said to her, "Wasn't this a fun weekend?"

"It sure was, Rafe."

"Gorgeous hotel," I remarked.

"It was okay," Jenny answered vaguely. "It wasn't as nice as the ones I stay at in Hawaii and New York, but it was okay."

It didn't hit me like a thunderbolt at first, but all during the drive back to L.A., I kept thinking about this little girl's reaction to our weekend. I thought I had done something unique; I had wanted these days to mean something special to these kids and I had worked very hard to put it together. Yet the simple truth was that these were fortunate children who didn't need me doing this for them.

I spent the next few weeks observing my co-workers. Some of them were very good teachers; others were at best adequate. The majority of them took the path of least resistance. They were working with kids who were practically on autopilot and they were quite content to lay out the school textbooks, follow along chapter by chapter, and go home to their soap operas and bridge games with their social lives in order and consciences clear. There's nothing wrong with this, of course, but it was wrong for me.

As I was the new kid on the block, they often invited me out to dinner, and I started to realize that junior-high peer pressure was nothing compared to the pressures on teachers in an elementary school. "We read our books this way." "We teach history this way." "Do things this way, Rafe, and you'll get along well here."

They were right. Not only would I get along well, but also, at a rich school, the parents give you expensive presents at Christmas and at the end of the year. I was being paid for something I enjoyed doing, and still had health insurance and three months a year off. That's a good gig, but I wasn't happy. I started losing sleep and coming to school with knots in my stomach. Finally I figured out why this was happening. Camelot was too pleased with itself. The kids were good, but they weren't *that* good. The school had a sort of 1950s feel to it, which was fine, but an occasional new idea was seen as a threat to the established order. Still, I never spoke up when I observed certain songs being sung or dances being performed, even though I knew I had ideas that might be better. I had learned my place. Unfortunately, I also learned, to my shock, that a few of my fellow teachers routinely cheated on standardized examinations to inflate test scores and build the school's reputation in the community.

Early in my first year, I attended a staff meeting at which standardized tests were the main topic of discussion. In those days, children in California took an exam known as the SES, or Survey of Essential Skills. It was a very easy test assessing the most basic abilities. Children at Camelot were encouraged to get 100 percent on this test, and were given a "100%" button to wear around school if they did so.

After the meeting, two highly respected teachers took me aside to show me a teaching technique that would help my students maximize their performance. This test was a multiple-choice exam for which the students blacked in the bubbles next to the answers on a computerized form. The teachers had a grid of bubbles that could be placed over a student's answer sheet, and this grid's holes revealed only the correct answers, so that a teacher could immediately spot how many questions had been missed. In some classes, when students announced they had finished their tests, they were told to come up to the teacher's desk. The teacher would use her grid and tell the student that he or she "had missed three—go back, find your mistakes, and return your paper again when you think you have 100 percent."

"Isn't that cheating?" I asked timidly.

"Of course not," one teacher replied testily. "I'm not telling the children the answer or which problem they missed— I'm simply encouraging them to get all the answers right. If they do, our school looks better when the scores are printed in the newspapers. And the higher our test scores, the more money we receive for various programs."

I was too intimidated to talk back to this veteran, but I did summon the nerve to bring it up with my principal when we were alone in his office. I told him I could never administer a test that way, and planned just to encourage the kids to do their best; when they missed answers, it simply meant that I would have to reteach those skills. I hoped that was okay.

My principal shook his head and said that while he knew

where I was coming from, he nevertheless was disappointed with my stubborn refusal to see the big picture. He said I had a lot to learn. I guess I did.

I learned one thing from testing my students honestly, though: I began to sleep better. I no longer had knots in my stomach when I came to school.

But I didn't have the wisdom or sense to articulate to myself that I was beginning to define my mission as a teacher. I didn't see the forest for the trees. Yet even in those early years, I was thinking a lot like Huck Finn, one of my heroes.

There's a marvelous section of Twain's great novel in which Huck is confronted with one of his many serious moral dilemmas. He has begun to feel guilty about helping Jim, a runaway slave, gain his freedom. As society has taught Huck to do, he decides to turn Jim in the first chance he gets. As their raft floats along, they come upon two men who capture runaway slaves for a living. Huck has his chance to betray Jim and follow the rules of society. Instead, at the last minute, he lies to the men and saves his friend.

Later, he feels even guiltier, believing he has done wrong. Yet, he thinks to himself, would he have felt better if he had turned Jim in and done right? As Huck says, "What's the use you learning to do right, when it's troublesome to do right and ain't no trouble to do wrong, and the wages is just the same? I was stuck. I couldn't answer that. So I reckoned I wouldn't bother no more about it, but after this always do whichever come handiest at the time."

Over the years, I've often applied Huck's logic in my classroom, and been the better for it. I do not eat in the teachers' lunchroom; instead, during recess and lunch I've struggled but managed to teach hundreds of children how to play guitar and other instruments. When my district assigns textbooks to the children that would cure the most seriously afflicted insomniac, I've used texts of my own choosing to inspire the children to dedicate themselves to their studies. While many teachers understandably go to after-school classes in order to earn credits leading to higher salaries, I've remained in my classroom for two hours a day after school to teach extra subjects.

As many new teachers will admit about themselves, I was completely incompetent during my first few years in the classroom, but at least I figured out one thing. With apologies to Paul Anka and Frank Sinatra, I was going to do it my way. I discovered I wasn't going to be happy living a life to please others. I needed to live a life helping others. I wanted to be in a school where children didn't go to hotels. I desired to go where children not only didn't own books but didn't even know where the local library was.

Sometimes fate deals you a good hand. As I was fretting over my unhappiness at Camelot, I coached the school's math team and it won a district championship. As I proudly left the scene of my team's glory, a principal from a school across town approached me. His team of youngsters had done very poorly that day, and I noticed them walking to their bus with their heads down.

This principal had heard about me from my current principal, who had complained about me at administrative meetings; my current leader had said I was a talented young man but "difficult to control." This gentleman from across town asked if I would like to transfer to his school, where the teaching would be tougher. But he promised to stay out of my way. It was an intriguing invitation. In his words, he was inviting me to leave Camelot and come to the Jungle, as he nicknamed his school. The man was shrewd—I have to admit it. He baited the hook and caught me easily. More important, he was totally honest about staying out of my way: the day I began at his school, he retired. I will never forget his wry smile and wink the day he stopped by my classroom to both greet me and say farewell.

So the following year I found myself in the Jungle, a school twenty minutes away from Camelot, though it might as well have been twenty light-years. The school was so crowded that students played handball at recess against classroom doors. Over two thousand children attended the school, and all were fed breakfast and lunch there every day. Practically no student tested at grade level. No one spoke English as a first language at home. The test scores were so low that I doubt cheating would have helped much.

Trying to replicate what little success I had had at my first school, I planned a weekend trip to the Shakespeare Festival in San Diego. During the orientation meeting for parents and children, there were only a few questions. Parents wanted to know if their children would need passports. Were the children going to be in danger from the INS for leaving Los Angeles? The children wanted to know if there were bathrooms and beds at the hotel. Would there be a telephone to enable them to call home? No one mentioned Hawaii.

And so I left the perfect school and perfect situation to go to a place where I have often failed, been hurt, and been downright miserable. It certainly hasn't been a picnic. But I have never regretted avoiding the path of least resistance. At first I didn't know how to negotiate this new course, but in the years to come I would discover many of the ways to stay it. One thing was certain: Robert Frost was a wise man.

CHAPTER 2

Who Are You?

It was fabulous being a young male teacher. I wasn't a very good one but was too ignorant to know it. The kids at Camelot had liked me and wanted to be in my class— after all, it was 1983 and I was the only teacher there who not only knew about Culture Club and the Clash but could play their music on my guitar. I was the teacher who was with it and could relate to the kids. And I was far too foolish in those early days to realize that teaching and parenting are not popularity contests. I had been the only male teacher at Camelot and there were plenty of pretty female teaching assistants. I don't need to draw you a picture, but the appreciation of the children and attention from good-looking women more than made up for the small paycheck.

When I came to the Jungle, the pattern continued with the teaching assistants, who were often interested in me because there was a Pied Piper quality to my teaching. I'm lucky enough to have charisma with children, and many of the women at school found that attractive. This fact, coupled with my recent reading of Bernard Malamud's fascinating novel *The Natural*, often led to conversations that got me what I was after.

In *The Natural*, Roy Hobbs is asked what he wants. In his best Ted Williams/Joe DiMaggio persona, Hobbs replies that he plays baseball so that one day, when he walks down the street, people would see him and say, "There goes Roy Hobbs—the best that ever played the game." I bought in to it completely. When asked by young women (and I was asked this a lot) why I had such passion and commitment to my students, I would reply, "Because one day, I want to walk down the street, and people will say, 'There goes Rafe—he's the best teacher I ever saw.' "

The funny thing was, the teaching assistants were as stupid as I was! This line impressed the hell out of them. Really, Rafe? You're going to be the best? Maybe you're the best at other things, too.

It was then I met someone different from the others. Pretty, yes, but smart as well, and very direct. She, too, was impressed by my charm with the children and my work ethic. She, too, wanted to know what motivated me to work that hard. So I told her about Roy Hobbs and my walk down the street, and I sat back with a big grin on my face and waited for this woman to be mine.

She laughed and replied, "That's the most moronic thing I ever heard!"

"Huh?" I gasped. Snappy comeback, don't you think?

She went on, "So this is about you, is it? You do this for yourself? The kids just happen to be there? Who cares what anyone thinks as you walk down the street? What difference does that make?"

Ouch! The remark hurt. But it was the truth. I really hadn't been considering my mission. I realized I loved Roy Hobbs but hadn't understood that his reasoning was just as foolish as mine. I decided to search for a new role model.

As stupid as I was, though, I will proudly admit to making one good decision in those days. That woman who shot me down so coldly needed to be dealt with. I needed to get even with her! No one gets the better of me! I'll show her!

And I did get even. I married her.

But marrying the incredible Barbara was not the end of a journey of self-discovery—it was the beginning. Any good teacher has to answer some short but difficult questions: What is your mission? What is it that children will learn from being in your class? What will they take away with them?

If you've ever seen the movie *Dead Poets Society,* you realize that you're supposed to feel touched at the end. Mr. Keating has been fired, and his students stand on their desks to show him love and support. Sorry, but the guy was a poor teacher: all he taught his students was to like him. His students are forced to sign a petition against him they know to be false, because they're afraid of being expelled from school. Had he been a good teacher, his students never would have allowed themselves to be forced to sign a petition. I mean, I love Robin Williams, but Mr. Keating was a lousy teacher.

I wanted to be a better one. I didn't know what my mission was yet; I just knew that Roy Hobbs wasn't going to be the guy to take me where I was going.

No teacher, even one who understands the importance of

defining a mission, develops one immediately. It takes years of successes and failures to truly and accurately find one's voice. Of course, it's perfectly understandable for a beginning teacher to struggle; his mission is solely to survive the day and please others. However, the good teachers eventually take their instruction to another level and consider what it is that they really want to accomplish.

My mission actually developed in two parts. After a few years of struggle in the Jungle, I was considered a very good teacher. My students enjoyed coming to school, and I was doing some creative things with literature and the arts. I was also using my love of mathematics to help the kids become better problem solvers, extending their thinking far beyond arithmetic. At assemblies, my class sang the best songs and some of the kids were learning guitar from me at lunchtime. And yes, we did go to the San Diego Shakespeare Festival at the end of each year and had a terrific time. The compliments poured in from the kids, parents, and other teachers. Yet something was missing.

I felt that my students were working harder than they had before, and the class was easily the hardest-working in the school, but I didn't think their work ethic was so extraordinary. They seemed too easily pleased with their efforts; if they got most of their arithmetic correct, they figured that was better than they had done the year before and they were off the hook. Despite their obvious improvement, I knew that one day these children of the Jungle would be out in the world competing against those I had once taught at Camelot. It would be no contest, and I couldn't get this point across to my new students.

As I looked at our world, I began to see why so many students avoid really difficult challenges. We have created a fast-food society, and our children are paying a terrible price for our country's success. We now have instant everything, including instant coffee to drink with our instant movies on DVD. We don't even have to leave the house to shop anymore; we have instant communication and can download our favorite music without going to a store to acquire it.

Everything has become too easy for our young people, and we make things worse by lying to them. We don't help them to face reality. Teachers and schools lie to children and their parents all the time. We have courses for middle-school students called "pre-algebra." Pre-algebra? This term is a euphemism. These students never mastered basic arithmetic and are not ready for algebra when others their age are. We don't have the courage to tell these kids that the course they are taking is really "Arithmetic for Students Who Are Behind."

We have books entitled *Algebra Made Easy*. Well, algebra isn't easy. Success at algebra takes hundreds of hours of hard work and disciplined study. I began to identify the problem the first year I decided to teach my sixth-graders algebra. They had mastered all of their arithmetic skills. They had a terrible time conquering algebra.

It wasn't a question of their abilities—they were intellectually ready. They had not, however, developed the mental toughness and attitude to attack difficult material and persevere until they conquered it. I lectured and cajoled them and did everything I could think of to inspire them to fight hard and reach higher. The kids went on being frustrated and defeated. It was hard to blame them. How could I expect an eleven-year-old to value excellence when mediocrity was the order of the day? I had to keep reminding myself that excellence is a relative term. I was just unable to help my students see that being the best reader in the Jungle wasn't going to get you very far when real life began.

This problem plagued me for weeks. I knew these kids could do more, and I wasn't satisfied. I started to get closer to my answer one day during a history lesson. We were reading the Declaration of Independence and were breaking down each of Thomas Jefferson's extraordinary phrases. After the children had deciphered "inalienable rights," we moved on to "life, liberty, and the pursuit of happiness."

I realized then where the problem lay. My students, and so many of our young people today, want a good life. They love (even if they don't always appreciate) liberty. They all want to be happy. But I realized that day that my class was a microcosm of what is wrong with so many of our nation's young people today.

What happened to *pursuit*? We aren't handed happiness. We're given an opportunity to *pursue* it. But how many children really pursue their dreams anymore? How can you go after things when you're sitting in front of a television set or computer screen? Now that I'd identified the problem, I needed to find the answer.

And then one night we went to a concert to hear Lynn Harrell play Dvořák's magnificent cello concerto at the Hollywood Bowl. After the concert, forty-five of my students were invited backstage to meet the world-renowned cellist. It was an amusing sight, as Harrell is six feet five and dwarfed my little sixth-graders. The kids were intimidated by his height, his fame, and his extraordinary ability. One of them, a beginning cellist, timidly asked Harrell the question that would come to define part of my class mission. Peter looked up and said shyly, "Mr. Harrell, how can you make music that sounds that beautiful?"

Lynn had the answer I had been looking for. "Well," he said as he squatted down to look Peter right in the eye, "there are no shortcuts."

The kids knew right at that moment that he had said something important and true. They glanced at me furtively, realizing that my wheels were spinning. I said nothing. It was Friday night, and everyone understood that Monday was going to be a new day. I was on a mission, and now I had a slogan to spur on the quest.

When class began fifty-odd hours later, I laid out a better plan. There was a banner stretched across the front of the room proclaiming THERE ARE NO SHORTCUTS. Yes, life isn't fair. Other kids have more money. Their English is better. Their parents are better connected. The American dream may be more of a reach for the children of the poor. But from that day on, the dream became closer, because that motto changed the way my students attacked their work. It brought a new approach to learning. If students across town were better readers, we would have to work longer, harder, and with more discipline. We decided to lengthen our school day. Our day began at 8:00 A.M., but some students decided they should come two hours early and begin at 6:00. Many did, and practically everyone was there by 6:30. They asked if they could start studying on Saturday mornings with me. They spoke of sacrifice. Perhaps they would have to turn off their television sets, miss their favorite shows, and put video games on hold. In *Tuesdays with Morrie,* the wise and dying teacher tells Mitch Albom that it isn't required for a person to buy in to the culture. My students came to the same conclusion, and with a corollary: they not only rejected the culture, they created one of their own.

One might guess that these children stopped being children, but nothing could be further from the truth. I've watched that scary scene, when children are asked to be smaller versions of adults. That wasn't what happened at all. These kids still loved to laugh, have water-balloon fights, and scream their heads off at an amusement park. But they also wanted to learn algebra, and they discovered that to reach the promised land of higher education, one had to do things the hard way. The algebra was no easier, but everyone in the classroom knew that eventually word problems would reveal their solutions and the mystery of equations would be solved. The long hours and willingness to sacrifice created in this group a mental toughness so powerful that no hurdle was too high or forbidding. When the end of the year came and the kids took their final exam in algebra, everyone passed a test that would have humbled most eighth- and ninth-grade students.

But there was no wild celebration, because the expression "There are no shortcuts" had become a part of this group, and they understood that one year of algebra was just a beginning. From the time they grasped its meaning, this simple phrase affected everything these children did. Their confidence soared, but it didn't shout out to the world. It was a quiet, determined confidence that years later has become a staple of the personality of my classrooms.

And speaking of years later, in 1993 I was invited to speak in Houston in front of some enthusiastic young people from Teach For America. A couple of my students came with me to talk to teachers about how we work. The kids performed some Shakespeare, and I spoke about my work and my mission. And I spoke about shortcuts. A fantastic thing happened that evening.

Two bright and charismatic young men approached me

after my talk. They had enjoyed my presentation and loved my students. Michael Feinberg and David Levin, graduates from Penn and Yale, saw something immediately: they realized that although I had received unusual recognition for my teaching, I was a very ordinary person. They saw that I was not unusually bright or insightful. They considered that they could be doing the same things with economically disadvantaged children in Houston that I was doing in Los Angeles. Within two years, they had opened a charter school known as KIPP, or Knowledge Is Power Program. And they adopted "There are no shortcuts" as their rallying cry.

Today, years later, the KIPP schools are a franchise all over the United States. Their branches in Houston and the Bronx have deservedly received national attention and praise. Their students, like the ones with whom I work, have used our mission statement to launch themselves on a path that too many of our young people avoid. And of course it's deeply gratifying to see terrific young teachers use some of my experiences to help them help so many students improve the quality of their lives.

But even more gratifying is to think back to that first group of students who learned algebra with me. Each was special, but Kevin stood out most of all. Kevin was an adorable little boy who rarely spoke. He had a terrible stutter. He was not only a nice young man; I thought he was brilliant. I checked his school records, but none of his previous teachers had written anything about him except that he was quiet. I was too ignorant to realize that there was much more going on in his life than I could have imagined.

I didn't screw up entirely, however. I was sensitive to Kevin's withdrawn personality, so I didn't give him a large speaking part in our Shakespeare play that year. He was a fine guitarist, so he anchored our band instead. I also began playing chess with him, and he was easily the best young chess player I had ever encountered. I thought we had a good year together. I enjoyed having him in class. But I did not see Kevin for almost four years after that.

One day I was sitting in our school auditorium. My class was on a vacation break, but they still came to school every day to study with me. Since it's a year-round school, our regular classroom was being occupied by another group of students. We gathered wherever there was floor space in the school to sit and read. The kids and I were reading *Animal Farm* when I looked up and saw Kevin.

He was much taller than he used to be, but still the same thin, shy, good-looking young man. His smile hadn't changed at all—Kevin never showed any teeth but merely curved his lips upward. He had a bouquet of flowers in one hand and a note in the other, and he handed both of these to me. He stuttered a hello to the kids and walked out.

I opened the note and recognized his handwriting from the days when he was in my class. He thanked me for being so good to him years before, and told me that he was doing well. He mentioned that he still played chess and really enjoyed it.

I didn't hear from him again for another two years. Then one day he came to my class and asked if he could help me out on Saturday mornings when I worked with former students—I had started SAT preparation classes for some ex-students now in middle and high school. He told me he felt he could be of service, as he himself had recently been preparing for college. I was thrilled to have him as an assistant. I knew so little about Kevin, but a few details came out as I worked with him that year.

He still stuttered, but his speech had improved. He was one of the finest high school chess players in the nation, regularly defeating top opponents from all over the country. He was the captain of his school chess team and his school science team. To top it all, he was one of the premier scorers in all of California in the competition known as the Academic Decathlon. This is an intense event in which teams of students from around the nation compete scholastically in a wide variety of subjects. These students train relentlessly for a year, often staying at their respective schools into the early morning hours.

There was an interesting story behind Kevin's participation with his school team. Before attending his current school, Kevin had been assigned to his neighborhood high school, an institution with a very poor reputation and typically low expectations for its students. This school was known, however, for a fine Academic Decathlon team. They had a chance, especially with Kevin on the team, to win the entire national championship. Kevin had participated as a tenth-grader and scored more points than the older students on the team. The coach desperately wanted Kevin to help him win a national championship.

Kevin didn't get along with his coach and left the school for one whose team wasn't a national contender but had a coach whose approach Kevin liked better. When Kevin was a senior, his team defeated his old school but won no national honors. Kevin won over a dozen medals at the state level, many of them gold. He also had a 4.5 GPA and scored 1540 on the SAT with a perfect 800 in mathematics. He was rejected by Stanford (I have never understood why) but was awarded a Regents' Scholarship by the University of California at Berkeley.

That's not too shabby for a boy with a serious stutter who barely spoke in sixth grade. Yet even with all these incredible accomplishments, Kevin did something that left me speechless during the last Saturday class of our year together. Throughout the year he had been modest, speaking quietly over the shoulders of students working through equations or reading-comprehension questions. Now, during the final class of the year, he asked me if he could address the class. It was very quiet in the room. Kevin has a soft voice and the students showed their respect for this remarkable young man by giving him their undivided attention.

He reminded the class that everyone has problems. He told the students that no one, including me, knew that when he was a small boy he faced severe problems at home. He spoke of never having enough money to do the things other kids at school were doing. He talked about the teachers who didn't believe in him, and began to cry when he said that it was my kindness and absolute certainty that he was special that had saved him. He insisted that the current students appreciate all they had in that little classroom. He talked of the pain of his family life, the frustration foolish teachers caused him, and the anger he felt when Stanford rejected him while accepting fellow students who had spent their high school years smoking dope and ditching classes, knowing their fathers' checkbooks would get them to places he was not allowed.

But, he told them, when you realize that life is often unfair, also remember that the world is an amazing place, and he begged them never to lose sight of the wonder of it all. He spoke of nature, beauty, and the miraculous potential of a human being with dreams.

When he was done, he asked if anyone had questions.

Most of the children couldn't speak and had tears welling up in their eyes. But then one of the children asked him how he had gotten through the beatings, hypocrisy, and cruelty of the world to win a Regents' Scholarship.

Kevin looked at me. "There are no shortcuts," he said.

It was a wonderful and awful moment for me. I have never loved another human being more than I loved that boy at that moment. Few people in the world are as strong and wise as he.

Yet I didn't know on that night the cellist first spoke those magic words that my mission was only half completed. The foundation was laid and was solid. Anguish and disheartening failure were yet to come.

CHAPTER 3

Johnny Can't Read

There are moments in our lives that we remember forever. We remember with dread our reaction to JFK's assassination. My daughter remembers the day she heard that Magic Johnson had contracted the AIDS virus. On a happier note, I remember the breathtaking moment that the best man I have ever known, my father, took me into our backyard and taught me how to throw a curveball. But I also remember the day I returned from school, not yet ten years old, to be told that cancer had killed him. I remember that Wednesday every day of my life.

I never forget a sound I heard on my first day as a teacher. It was the sound of fifth-graders groaning.

Why did they groan? Was it a bad joke? Bad food? Bad smell? A physical ailment? No. They groaned when I told them it was time for reading.

Why did these kids hate to read? And why are so many children inferior readers? Educators and parents, social scientists, and members of the media constantly grapple with this question, and there are all kinds of solutions offered to help Johnny read.

The blame doesn't lie in one place. With such a complicated and crucial part of a child's education in jeopardy, there are many forces at work—a sort of conspiracy of mediocrity that denies children the chance to develop a love of reading and become good readers. It is a pattern that involves our system, parents, teachers, and sometimes even librarians.

Please don't be upset. I see the letters coming in already. Yes, I know there are outstanding teachers, librarians, parents, and others who work hard and care deeply about the literacy of our children. Yet if this is so, why is it that so many of our nation's children read so poorly? It is because for each one of these terrific people, there are others who interfere with or water down the good work that they do. I have had success with my students, and successful educators must share their vision and experience if America is to escape the fall many of us see coming sooner than any of us want to admit.

I am a regular classroom teacher. I am a president of absolutely nothing. I sit on no committees, attend no meetings, and I don't want to. Most people who make teaching suggestions couldn't teach a group of students on their best day. They are sales representatives from companies with an economic, not an educational, agenda. I was in my classroom at six o'clock this morning and will be there at six tomorrow morning. And when I tell my students to get ready for literature, they cheer. You, as a parent or teacher, can have the same results. But the journey will not be an easy one, given the world in which we live.

Let's face it: reading is the most important subject in school. It's more important than all the other subjects combined. If a child can't learn to read well and love to read, the chances of that kid finding success and happiness on any level are low. I have watched hundreds of students leave my fifth-grade classroom and go on to accomplish remarkable things. These successful kids represent the spectrum of racial, religious, economic, and cultural diversity in the United States, but they have one thing in common: they read well and love it. My journey to get to this point, however, has not been easy, and it will never get any easier.

It's easy to become angry when you teach. Having finished UCLA, I taught at Camelot for two years and mistakenly believed I was a good teacher. But there were a few things I did well. One smart move I made was to throw out the basal readers my students had been using.

Many elementary kids hate these books, and I don't blame them. The stories are boring, and worse still, the books come with hundreds of worksheets to be xeroxed by the teacher to teach the kids "skills." Most teachers divide their class into reading groups based on the skill level of the children. When the children aren't reading with the teacher, they spend quiet time in the class filling out the sheets. The only purpose of this work is to keep kids occupied while the teacher is reading with another group. The kids don't learn any skills from doing these sheets (just ask them), and more importantly, they begin to loathe reading.

I got rid of state-sponsored books. They killed the joy reading is supposed to give. Instead, I began reading literature with the children. We read Mark Twain and John Steinbeck. We read Charles Dickens and Maya Angelou. At Camelot the kids were ready to read these authors with me. These kids all had two parents. They all spoke English. When I mentioned that they might like reading John Steinbeck's *The Pearl*, many of them had a copy at home that an older brother had read. Mothers went to the bookstore to buy their kids a copy, or the kids themselves pedaled over to the library to check out the book. Things were going well. The children loved to read and their parents were very happy.

Things were different two years later when I arrived at the Jungle. None of the children spoke English at home. A large percentage of these kids were below the poverty level, and that economic fact meant few books in their homes.

As I mentioned, it's easy to become angry. When I met my new fifth-grade class, I could see right away that these children were just as bright as the children I had taught at Camelot. But English was not their first language, and there were no ballet lessons after school. These children couldn't read well in *any* language.

I was upset, but I knew I could fix this. I announced that we were going to read literature to help them develop a love of reading. I told them we were going to read Steinbeck's *Of Mice and Men* beginning the next week, and explained to them how they could get a copy of the book.

However, none of these children knew where a bookstore was located. None of them knew where the *library* was located, and none of them had a library card.

Now I was getting angrier, but I was determined. I said to myself, I'll get the class copies of the Steinbeck this Saturday. I checked my phone book and looked up a dozen public libraries within about a twenty-mile radius of my apartment. Some opened at 9:00 A.M. and others at 10:00. I planned my route Friday night and figured I could borrow thirty-six copies of *Of Mice and Men* and be home by one in the afternoon. Hey, the UCLA football game was on, and I don't miss UCLA football games.

Things began well enough. I went to my local library at nine that Saturday morning in search of John Steinbeck's *Of Mice and Men,* and I hit pay dirt! This particular library had six copies. This was going to be easier than I thought. Then I went to check the books out.

I placed the six books on the desk and set my library card on top of them.

Rafe: Good morning. How are you today?

Librarian: Fine, thank you. What do you think you're doing?

Rafe: Oh, I guess this does look funny. I'm a teacher and my class is reading this book.

Librarian: You can't check out six books.

Rafe: Well, sure I can. That's a teacher's card there. The rule is you can check out up to ten books for a month.

Librarian: Ten different books.

Rafe: Huh?

Librarian: Ten different books. It's obvious, isn't it? If you check those out, there won't be any left. We want those six books read by six different people.

Rafe: Six different people will *be reading them! Six* different *kids.*

Librarian: Look, that's not the same thing and you know it. I don't need troublemaking teachers screwing up the rules. You may check out one and one only.

Now I was *really* angry, and in shock. Troublemaking teacher? I had looked forward to help from supportive librarians. Then I decided that this lady was the exception and not the rule. Well, I got the same story and treatment at every library I entered.

Still, a creative and dedicated teacher cannot be stopped. I learned quickly. In the weeks to come, I would go into libraries to check out books for the kids, then return an hour later in disguise, with a change of clothes, glasses, a hat, and sometimes even a fake mustache. And I got all the copies of books I needed.

The point here is that even when the system is against you, if you're a good teacher you'll do anything and everything to get books into the hands of your students. But it's obvious why so many potentially fine teachers give up. Our job is tough enough without so many unnecessary and ridiculous hurdles being placed our way.

Things were good and getting better. During my first year at the Jungle, I fired up my students. They read a lot of interesting and enjoyable books with me and loved every minute of it. We had a hilarious *Alice in Wonderland* day. After we finished the story, the kids came to school dressed as their favorite characters. One boy was such a convincing Alice (great blue dress and makeup, courtesy of a terrific mom) that he was thrown out of the boys' bathroom when he had to go during recess! We read Mark Twain and Richard Wright. We read George Orwell. Test scores went way up. The children were happy. Their parents were thrilled. And I was ecstatic—at least for a short while.

A year later, the librarian at the local junior high school, where most of these students went after graduating from the fifth grade, paid me a visit. She was very upset with me. I had ruined her program. In her own words, my students had read "too many books."

She wasn't kidding. She also yelled at me for reading the "wrong books." You couldn't read *The Pearl* with fifth-graders because it was listed as an eighth-grade book. Well, how can you argue with intelligent, thoughtful criticism like that?

Sorry to be sarcastic, but this was incredible to me. Here was a *librarian*, for God's sake, who was more concerned with her list than the fact that she had kids who read well and wanted to read more. And as a foolish young teacher, I let my anger get the better of me. I voiced my disgust to her and made a suggestion that I believe, unless one is incredibly limber and talented, is physically impossible to follow.

I was wrong, of course, to say such a thing. Later on, as you will read, I found the role model to inspire me to handle such situations with more grace, maturity, and, most important of all, results.

But the warning is here for all you young teachers who dare to be first-rate—there will be many who will try to stop you. Outstanding teaching will require you not only to do everything in your power to reach your students but to battle forces that are supposed to be on your side. You may be lucky and wind up in that rare school or district where those in charge support your efforts. However, it's not unusual for people more concerned with money, politics, and power to hinder the efforts of dedicated teachers. So be prepared for battle, unless you want to be like everyone else.

And believe me, it's even harder for parents. You're at home putting your trust in people who are supposed to be inspiring your child to become a thinker. Please stay involved, because there are teachers who will do nothing to deserve your confidence. Here is a case in point.

It may seem obvious, but one of the reasons Johnny can't read is that we're hiring teachers who aren't competent. Large urban school districts are desperate for teachers; they hire practically anyone with a pulse. Many of these young teachers actually work quite hard, but unfortunately working hard doesn't necessarily make someone an effective teacher.

Frankly, you need to be fairly smart to be a good teacher. At the elementary school level, a good teacher not only knows literature and some mathematics but must also be versed in basic science, history, and the arts, as well as being equipped to play social worker and psychologist. Many of the people we hire are not up to this level, and the children are not the only ones who suffer—the parents do, too.

After many years of teaching I began to receive some national attention for the work my students were doing, and people began coming from all over to observe and perhaps get some ideas they could use in their own classrooms. Here is the story of two young fifth-grade teachers who came to watch me teach reading.

They both told me their students hated reading. They had heard that my students loved to read, and read very well. For a week they watched me teach. As it happened, we were reading *Of Mice and Men*.

The kids did a fabulous job understanding George and Lennie. I thought this particular class was especially insightful in seeing that Lennie, Crooks, and Candy were all outcasts in a harsh and unforgiving time. At the end, the children broke down and cried when George killed Lennie, they had come to love them both so much. The children wrote intelligently about the book, and on the Friday we finished, they spoke eloquently in class about the value of true friendship.

That night I took the two teachers out to dinner. Our conversation went something like this:

Rafe: Well, thanks for spending the week. I hope you got some ideas.

Teacher 1: Well, I could never read that book with my students.

Rafe: Really?

Teacher 1: It has that word in it.

Rafe: What word?

Teacher 1: You know. The D word.

Rafe: Dog?

Teacher 1: You know very well what I mean. [whispers] "Damn."

Rafe: To tell you the truth, I think my students have heard that word before. But your point is well taken. The issue here isn't for you to read something that you find distasteful. I've chosen literature I personally love, and in teaching it, my passion is passed on to my students. You can do the same thing. Tell me a book that has meant something to you.

Teacher 1: Well, I don't like to read. I never read.

It wasn't easy, but I was able to keep my spaghetti in my mouth and not spit it all over the table. This kind of thing has happened over and over again. Many young teachers don't read at all. How can we expect them to help our children become good readers?

It can get worse. The other teacher visiting my classroom decided to use *Of Mice and Men* in class and invited me to watch a lesson. I was horrified as this young man explained to his fifth-graders that Steinbeck was teaching us George was a very evil man who would burn in hell forever because of his murderous act. I'm not kidding.

When I spoke with this young man later, I tried as gently as possible to suggest to him that he had missed the point of the story. "No, I didn't," he snapped at me, "because it's my interpretation."

And this man still teaches today. That's a frightening thought. I shudder to imagine his interpretation of *The Diary of Anne Frank*. So, parents, know what is happening in your classroom. If the teacher is not inspiring your child to read unforgettable works of literature, it's probably true that you won't be able to do much about what is happening in the classroom. However, your knowledge that the teacher is doing a poor job can help you repair the damage at home. That's not fair to you, of course, but working with your child helps him or her be a better reader.

Don't despair. We can still develop ardent readers who love good books. But first, now that we've heard a few horror stories about teachers, let's not forget the role some of our school districts and administrators play in preventing Johnny from reaching the promised land.

Every few years the bureaucrats who run school districts try to fix things. Here in Los Angeles, our test scores are so low it's embarrassing. And the powers that be have come up with the solution: Open Court Reading. Open Court is a basal reader that comes with a comprehensive teacher guide. The lessons are scripted with a rigid structure. All teachers are supposed to set up their classrooms in the same way, hang the posters the company gives you on the same walls of each classroom, and every child at a particular grade level is supposed to finish each unit at the same pace. A child in the fifth grade at one school should be on the same unit as a fifth-grader at a school across town. Everyone in our district will read these books. The children's reading speed and comprehension are frequently assessed.

I have met caring administrators who admit that this system has its flaws. They know that a "one size fits all" approach to reading is ridiculous, because in reality, one size *doesn't* fit all. Yet these officials have pointed out to me that for many of our young teachers, a carefully scripted series of reading lessons will help, as the teachers are new and don't know what to do. And teachers who don't read on their own will be forced to read these scripted lessons with their students, because they will look bad if their students perform poorly on the frequent assessments.

There is truth to this, but the proponents of systems like Open Court have made the fatal mistake of surrendering to failure. They are saying, "Our kids can't read, our teachers are not always qualified, and though this system isn't very good, it may improve things a little bit and raise a few test scores."

If that's your approach, go for it. I, however, want my students to be outstanding readers who know that Malcolm X and Alex Haley wrote a brilliant book and didn't just own a T-shirt company. Basal readers like Open Court will never bring children to this level.

One last frightening effect of this new system is that everyone is supposed to teach it for two and a half hours each morning. I have already met many teachers who have stopped teaching science and social studies altogether. The idea is that since they will be judged by reading and math scores, they needn't worry about the other subjects, since the children won't be tested on them at the end of the year. Thus, we have not only lost our focus on why we teach Johnny to read, but in the process we've eliminated other subjects so that Johnny can't even get the chance to learn science, geography, and history.

But, my friends, all is not lost. You can still have a child who one day will ask for a certain book for Christmas or a birthday. I certainly do not have all the answers, but here are a few tips to teachers and parents who want their children to be excited every time they go to the library.

Choose material you personally love.

Read your favorite books with your students; they will respond to your enthusiasm for the material. Remember: the goal is to demonstrate the joy of reading; the material used is less important than the teacher's level of excitement.

This is also true for parents. I know many excellent parents who read to their children when the kids are young but stop when the children arrive in elementary school because they feel the children will get all the necessary reading lessons they need there. They won't.

Personally, I love Mark Twain, John Steinbeck, William Shakespeare, Richard Wright, George Orwell, and Charles Dickens, and I always read their best works with my fifth-graders. However, this doesn't mean that *you* should read *Animal Farm*. I have a colleague who loves C. S. Lewis's *Chronicles of Narnia* and bases quite a lot of his reading program on his love for that material. And his kids are good readers.

Many teachers I know have brought literature into their classrooms but tell their students to "Go home and read this chapter" or "Finish the chapter we started tonight." With difficult literature, this is an ineffective and lazy strategy. Some kids will struggle through, but many won't do the assignment and others will be turned off what could be an important experience for them. *You* are the catalyst for a successful program and must go through the difficult material with the kids. That's why you get paid big money!

I don't have a desk in the classroom. I'm on my feet, like Henry V exhorting his soldiers to fight on St. Crispin's Day. I've spent hours planning what chapters we will read. I know which passages I'll read aloud and which will be read by the students. I know which child will handle the challenge of the most difficult paragraphs, and I carefully plan an easy passage for a shy youngster who needs success to begin his journey as a good reader. Nothing is left to chance. My reading lesson is like an orchestra, and as the conductor, I have the job to make the instruments sing. I know when to stop reading and ask challenging questions. It takes enormous energy, but to be in a room with young minds who hang on every word of a classic book and beg for more if I stop makes all the planning worthwhile. The reading hour provides me with my happiest moments as a teacher: the children's gasps when Pip discovers that Magwitch is his benefactor, their delighted shock as they hide in the apple barrel with Jim Hawkins over-hearing Long John Silver, their sobs when George kills Lennie, their joyous laughter as Tom hoodwinks his com-rades into whitewashing the fence, and their deafening silence when Atticus leaves the courtroom are vindication of my struggle to help my students make their lives extraordinary.

Once a child leaves your classroom, she is bombarded by powerful distractions that will keep her from pursuing excellence. Whether it's the latest video game, television, or the Internet, most children today don't have the strength to resist the distractions that have been carefully orchestrated by people who don't care about your child. Children need plenty of adult guidance to become good readers.

Parents can provide this at home. If you're reading *James and the Giant Peach* with your child, have two copies and trade off reading paragraphs to each other. Even if your child can read it by himself, the joy of reading with a loved one and discussing and sharing feelings is crucial in the development of a good reader as well as a nice human being. Sadly, there's a good chance your child is not getting this kind of training in the classroom. In any event, reading at home with you, the parent, will dramatically increase the odds that your child will be an excellent reader. Society is filled with forces of mediocrity that are going to battle you for the potential that is within your child. Your time and energy are the greatest weapons against those forces.

If you are a young teacher, remember not to allow outside pressures or political correctness to determine your reading program. When I first came to the Jungle, a religious fanatic brought some parents to my classroom. He had heard that the kids were reading *The Diary of Anne Frank* and told me that this book was too controversial for a classroom. He then gave me a typed list of all the books he and his group felt should be banned from schools. I thanked him very much. He had created a reading list for the entire year!

Here are my favorite books to read with my fifth-graders:

Of Mice and Men (John Steinbeck)
The Adventures of Tom Sawyer (Mark Twain)
The Adventures of Huckleberry Finn (Mark Twain)
The Autobiography of Malcolm X (as told to Alex Haley)
Native Son (Richard Wright)
The Joy Luck Club (Amy Tan)
Bury My Heart at Wounded Knee (Dee Brown)
Treasure Island (Robert Louis Stevenson)

We follow a reading of Stevenson's classic with an all-day treasure hunt. The kids come to school dressed as pirates and follow a difficult series of clues leading them all over the building in search of a map. The map then leads them to a spot where they have to dig up a treasure chest. What's inside the buried chest? Books!

A Christmas Carol (Charles Dickens)
Great Expectations (Charles Dickens)
Night (Elie Wiesel)
The Diary of a Young Girl (Anne Frank)
To Kill a Mockingbird (Harper Lee)

do with a sense of excellence. Our children today are not reading as well as they should, and it's not because of their abilities—it's because we don't read with them as often and with the intensity needed to develop fine young minds.

Yes, I know—parades and celebrations develop self-esteem. But self-esteem without skills is a hollow accomplishment. I want my students to have the chance to attend an outstanding university one day. When a student interviews at Stanford, is the university more impressed with his reading comprehension or his ability to do a fan dance? Let's hope he can do both, but first things first.

We read every day. Show me a good reader, and I'll show you a child with strong self-esteem.

*Make a connection between your program
and the outside world.*

My enthusiasm for the subject motivates my students to read well. In addition, I link a future activity to the classroom. For example, when Sir Ian McKellen did a world tour of *Richard III,* all the students who read it with me got to attend a performance. We read *Hamlet* and followed it by going to see the film with Kenneth Branagh. Teachers who like reading the *Harry Potter* books with their students can follow up with a trip to the movies, and for the really adventurous, you can join my students and me when we go to see *The Lord of the Rings.* Why not? They've all read Tolkien!

Remember, there are no shortcuts. Some teachers choose marvelous works of literature but don't go deep enough to show the students *why* the work is classic. My students are taught to understand that Huck's journey is their journey, too. My students cry when Huck decides, "All right, I'll go to Hell." They relate to him because I have helped them make the connection to their own journeys. There are teachers who teach particular books because they're following a required reading list, but they may not prepare or really know the material they're teaching. Recently, former students of mine told me about their seventh-grade English class. Their teacher had them read *A Midsummer Night's Dream* but pronounced Titania "Ty-tay-nee-uh" and became upset when the students tried to correct her. When they explained that Bottom and Pyramus were the same character and thus should be read by only one student, she collected the books and canceled their Shakespeare unit.

A group of former students told me that they were reading *The Crucible* in their eighth-grade English class. These students now attend a famous and respected private school, yet they were never taught about the Salem witch trials. Their teacher didn't explain to them the larger meaning of Arthur Miller's play involving the McCarthy era and witch-hunts, she simply gave the kids the book and told them it was a famous and important play.

You as the teacher or parent must do better than that. If you want your students to maximize their reading potential, you must lead by example. It starts with you. Make your reading program thrilling, challenging, and, equally important, relevant.

Lives hang in the balance. If you do nothing else as a teacher, develop able and passionate readers.

CHAPTER 4

I Won't Back Down

What do you stand for? My father taught me that a person who stands for nothing will fall for anything. The best teachers stand for a set of principles on which they will not compromise.

Unfortunately, teachers frequently march over cliffs, lemminglike, when given instructions from administrators. Teachers grumble when they notice unfairness or foolishness, but far too often they go along because they're afraid. Well, I teach fifth grade, but I'm not *in* the fifth grade. To be an effective teacher, one sometimes has to stand one's ground even at the risk of angering administrators. On most issues I'm willing to compromise to survive; compromise is essential to the success of any large institution. However, on the following issues, I won't back down. I hope young teachers will understand the issues essential to their own effectiveness: on these issues they should dig in their heels.

There are no shortcuts.

When parents of children who attend one of the private schools on the West Side of Los Angeles notice that their children are having trouble with a subject, they understand that studying with a paid tutor will improve the child's performance. Parents of poor children cannot hire tutors. They cannot afford after-school enrichment programs. To help students bring their academic performance up to the level of their wealthier contemporaries, I have extended the number of school days and lengthened the hours each day so that they have more time to practice the skills that bring academic success. There was nothing magic about Magic Johnson. He became a great basketball player not only because of his colossal talent but also because he spent thousands of lonely hours perfecting his craft through discipline and enormously hard work.

America should be the land of equal opportunity. Does any sane person believe that this is true for a child growing up in poverty? Many students are terrific kids with outstanding abilities, but they come from poor areas plagued with crime. Many of them are fatherless. Many live with people who have drug, alcohol, or other emotional problems. Some kids don't have either parent at home and are being raised by relatives or friends. Their guardians often don't speak English. Older siblings may be involved with gangs and drugs. How can I, as their teacher, level the playing field for these kids? It becomes level when they understand *There Are No Shortcuts*.

I challenge them with what some would call a grueling schedule of hard work and study from 6:30 A.M. until 5:00 P.M. They come to class during their vacations and often work with me at my house on Saturday afternoons. The regular school schedule provides approximately sixteen weeks of vacation a year, based on the old farm calendar when children needed to help their families harvest crops. My students have no crops to harvest, nor do they have summer homes, summer camp, or private lessons to occupy them during vacations. Their choice is between my classroom, a tiny cell where they live, or the streets. My room is where they find a chance to catch up to their wealthy peers. No, I don't get paid for the extra work. Someone has to do *something,* and perhaps someday the politicians who claim an interest in education will recognize that the way to improve math and reading, without sacrificing science, history, art, and music, is to extend the amount of time students spend in school. Meanwhile, based on my belief that *There Are No Shortcuts* and the knowledge that my students have been dealt a lousy hand, here is the daily schedule for my fifth-grade students:

6:30 A.M.	Students Arrive
	Math Team (problem solving, spatial relations, mental math, estimation)
8:00	Written Language (English grammar)
8:30	Mathematics
9:30	Literature
10:30	United States History
11:00	Recess (students have the option to stay in and learn to play guitar)

11:20	Science
12:00	World Geography and Economics
12:30	Lunch (optional guitar lessons continue)
1:20	Fine Arts
2:20	Physical Education
2:58	Regular school is dismissed
3:00	Shakespeare
4:00	Study Hall (students may stay or leave for home)
6:00	Last students leave

Teachers may choose not to follow this particular schedule, but extending class past the traditional time boundaries not only gives more teaching time but also sends an important message to students. The teacher, by example, is telling the kids that school counts, that school is an important place, and that education is the key that will open the door to a better future. Yes, the work is hard, but if a compassionate and caring teacher with a sense of humor leads the lessons, the kids will work enthusiastically and amaze everyone with their accomplishments.

The rest of our school currently begins at 8:00 A.M. and ends at 3:00 P.M. My students are in class at least three hours a day more than the other students, and this doesn't include the vacation and Saturday hours they work. The average student at my school will spend approximately 150 hours each year receiving arithmetic instruction. The students in my class will receive over 400. Students at the Jungle will read with a teacher for 200 hours each year, at the most. My students will read for more than 500 hours with me. You don't have to be Piaget to predict the results.

UCLA basketball coach John Wooden says: "The four laws of learning are explanation, demonstration, imitation, and repetition. The goal is to create a correct habit that can be produced instinctively under great pressure. To make sure this goal was achieved, I created eight laws of learning: namely, explanation, demonstration, imitation, repetition, repetition, repetition, repetition, and repetition."

There's a funny story regarding this belief of mine. In 1992 I took my class, as I always do, on a trip to Disneyland. This trip is used as a teaching tool far beyond the joy of visiting the Magic Kingdom. The kids spend two days there, staying in a hotel. They learn to handle and budget money, pay bills, and organize eating and sleeping arrangements in order to prepare for longer trips we'll be taking during the year. It's a valuable experience for them.

After two days and sixty rides, the kids were tired but happy as we boarded a van and several cars to make the thirty-mile trip back to Los Angeles. When our caravan got off the Santa Monica Freeway for the final few miles of the trip, our vehicles were attacked by mobs in the street. What the hell was going on?

Having been at Disneyland, we hadn't listened to any news for two days. Had we done so, we would have known that the verdicts had been rendered regarding the police beatings of Rodney King, and the shocking (but perhaps not surprising) not-guilty decisions had been declared. Many people's passions were inflamed, and Los Angeles was going to be as well.

The van and cars made it through the crowds with the kids lying on the floor, and they managed to arrive home safely. Although our class was officially on vacation, all the kids were due at school the following day to work on problem-solving skills and continue reading *The Autobiography of Malcolm X*. I hadn't planned it that way, of course, but reading Malcolm X when the neighborhood was on fire did bring a rather extraordinary intensity to this already brilliant book.

At 7:00 A.M. my class showed up in the school library, as other students who were officially in session were using our classroom. The school was mostly empty; many parents were keeping their children at home that day. In addition, many of the staff members had stayed home. By 10:00 A.M. the word was out on the street that our block was going up in flames that night, and everyone was clearing out of our school. I, however, had the students continue to work on solving problems. I have never claimed to be rational.

Finally, one student looked out the window of the library and mentioned to me that he could see buildings across the street on fire. He wanted to know if we were planning to leave soon, because the school was basically deserted.

"But Manuel," I told him, "math is very important. Remember, there are no shortcuts."

Manuel shot back, "That may be, Rafe, but let me tell you something—I'm taking a shortcut *outta here*!"

We left school, but I figured we were making progress. After all, if under siege the kids were using my motto to make a point, it's getting through, right?

I have high expectations.

Many teachers attempt to define success by lowering expectations so that all the students reach some can't-miss objective. At a local middle school, my former students have had teachers who skip reading books and show a film version of the work instead. A film is a nice supplement but can never be a substitute. Does everything have to be watered down? If we want to teach our students about Monet's paintings, do we have to repaint them with MTV logos around the frame so that the students can relate to his work? Of course not. Our students are capable of reaching into Monet's world if we show them the path.

Our standards in public schools are incredibly low. George Orwell would recognize modern administrators who rewrite history, moving the finish line so it coincides with the point where the kids happen to end up. Recently, my school celebrated its reading scores, which were twenty points lower than the national average. We celebrated being far below average! Many of the teachers were encouraged by the fact that our scores were a point or two higher than the dismal performance of a year earlier. Well, maybe it's important to look for the good and be optimistic, but delusion is not the answer. Those who celebrate failure will not be around to help today's students celebrate their jobs flipping burgers.

Teaching reading is not rocket science. Successful classrooms are run by teachers who have an unshakable belief that the students can accomplish amazing things and who *create the expectation that they will*. My students perform Shakespeare because I believe they can, *because they know that last year's class did, because I explain to them how they will do it and then I show them*. As soon as they master the first page, they begin to develop confidence in themselves. *They raise their own expectations*. A sad reality is that usually, when a teacher remarks that his class "can't understand this math or that literature," it is actually an assessment of the teacher's abilities and not those of the students. It may shock visitors to watch my fifth-graders perform an entire Vivaldi concerto from memory, but it doesn't shock me. I expect it.

Someone has to raise the bar, and that person is the teacher. If fifth-grade students are reading at a first-grade level, placing first-grade books in front of them will never help them catch up with the students across town who not only are in higher-achieving classrooms but have parents and tutors helping them every step of the way. Someone has to tell children if they are behind, and lay out a plan of attack to help them catch up. If this means staying after school or taking extra hours sitting with the child and reading, so be it. There are no excuses. Students new to the country or living with economic hardship are just as capable of becoming top students as their more privileged peers in other parts of the city. However, they will never get there if the teacher doesn't believe this. Children need and deserve our belief in their ability to improve skills. I constantly encourage my students to reach higher. Not a day goes by when I don't tell them that I'm not smarter than they are, only more experienced. I try to inspire them by reminding them of where they once were and how assignments that were once difficult have become easier due to their willingness to practice their skills with discipline. They have confidence because I build it in them.

If we want our students to explore new worlds, we must demand that they make the journey—not everything has to be spoon-fed to them. I don't have to give them an abridged version of *Hamlet*. Here is a poem that I was given by a friend of mine. It comes from Charles Osgood of CBS News, and it has become the centerpiece of my demand for Great Expectations.

Pretty Good

There once was a pretty good student,
Who sat in a pretty good class;
Who was taught by a pretty good teacher,
Who always let pretty good pass—

He wasn't terrific at reading,
He wasn't a whizbang at math;
But for him education was leading
Straight down a pretty good path.

He didn't find school too exciting,
But he wanted to do pretty well;
And he did have some trouble with writing,
And no one had taught him to spell.

When doing arithmetic problems,
Pretty good was regarded as fine—
5 plus 5 needn't always add up to be 10
A pretty good answer was 9.

The pretty good class that he sat in
Was part of a pretty good school;
And the student was not the exception,
On the contrary, he was the rule.

The pretty good student, in fact, was
Part of a pretty good mob;
And the first time he knew that he lacked was
When he looked for a pretty good job.

It was then, when he sought a position,
He discovered that life could be tough—

And he soon had a sneaking suspicion,
Pretty good might not be good enough.

The pretty good town in our story
Was part of a pretty good state,
Which had pretty good aspirations,
And prayed for a pretty good fate.

There once was a pretty good nation,
Pretty proud of the greatness it had,
Which learned much too late, if you want to be great,
Pretty good is, in fact, pretty bad.

I separate church and state.

It's Friday afternoon, so most kids are happy. They've worked hard all week and are looking forward to Saturday morning off (they're coming to my house for a music rehearsal Saturday afternoon, but they love playing).

Alex, however, seems sad. Many of the kids have organized their things and are off for home or perhaps to play a little baseball before the sun sets over the playground. Alex has stayed behind to help me clean up. I ask him what's bothering him. Doesn't he want to join his friends outside?

"They're not there," he replies morosely.

It seems that many of Alex's close friends have been invited by a former teacher to go to something the kids call VBS, or Vacation Bible School. Alex's teacher last year constantly proselytized her students to share in her religious beliefs. She gave up on Alex because he's a Jehovah's Witness.

Like almost all teachers I know who bring religion into

the classroom, she has the best of intentions. In fact, she's a very good teacher. Teachers like this don't mean to hurt the kids, but their personal passions can turn off some potentially terrific students.

Over the years, I learned from Alex, and from other students from other schools, that they have had teachers try to force religions on them. David, a particularly bright boy and a passionate atheist, recalled former instructors calling him names and insulting him when he challenged them for confusing religious beliefs with historical fact. He became particularly incensed when one teacher taught her fourth-graders that AIDS was God's way of punishing gay people. Another boy was more hurt than angry. He was an immigrant whose teacher had excluded him from a party at her house because he read the Koran at home instead of the Bible. She told him that the Koran was false and the Bible true. Later, she wrote on his report card that he was withdrawn and reluctant to participate in class.

This goes on far too frequently in too many schools. It's understandable, of course; religion is practically impossible to separate from oneself. Our beliefs are a large part of who we are, and it's natural to want to share those beliefs with young people.

But I don't. It's just too complicated. Most of the teachers in my school practice some sort of Christianity (although I think Jesus would be hard-pressed to recognize some of the things teachers have done in his name). The problem is that many students in our school are being raised at home as Hindus, Buddhists, Muslims, or Jews. Certainly, it's good for the children to know that others have different beliefs, and to celebrate diversity. However, when a teacher takes some students who agree with her to church and leaves others behind, the message is that "my way is the right way." I'm not wise enough to know the right way on religion, so I follow Thomas Jefferson and keep religion out of my public school classroom. This does not mean that morality and matters of character are not attended to; indeed, these issues often dominate the day. I just make sure that everyone is invited to the party. There are no infidels in my classroom.

I teach in English.

Very few children in our large public school speak English at home. Most come to school speaking practically no English at all, which brings us to the subject of bilingual education, a topic that can start an argument faster than abortion.

I have terrific teacher friends on both sides of this discussion. Unlike the more hysterical antagonists on this issue, I believe neither that people who favor teaching children in their native language are trying to destroy America, nor that people who oppose this practice are racists trying to destroy a people's history and culture.

Personally, for what it's worth, I think it's fine that children beginning school spend part of their day learning in their own language as they become acclimated to the American system. At its best, such a system allows a child to learn two languages. Unfortunately, because of poor teaching and poor home environments, the children do not become acclimated to our system and are not fluent in any language. As a fifth-grade teacher I regularly get students who have been at our school for five years and are not close to proficiency in English. If they aren't fluent in English at the end of fifth grade, they'll go on to middle school far behind children from other parts of town. As a result of our concern with diversity, we don't insist that students become fluent in English. Does anyone believe that putting them at a permanent disadvantage is a plus in their lives?

Looking down the road, how in the world can a child who isn't fluent in English do well on college entrance exams? Students who don't speak English will have no chance; this is why I teach in English.

I don't want to rob a child of his past. I encourage the children to speak their native languages at home. I praise them for it. I honor their cultures and teach them that being bilingual makes them truly well educated. But I also don't want to rob them of their future. In my experience, almost all non-English-speaking parents want their children to learn English. These parents have had doors closed in their faces because of their lack of English skills.

One of the sad facts about our school's bilingual problems is that we now hire teachers because they can speak a particular language to address a certain population of students. However, many of these teachers can barely speak English themselves. My students laugh when we walk down the hallway of our school and read signs put on the bulletin boards by these teachers. *"One day you can be a astronaught."* *"I'ts important to read."* *"Look at our grammer work."* I have not made these up—they are posted in my school and, no doubt, many others. While I appreciated my students' amusement, how can we expect a system that hires the poorly educated to produce excellence in education?

English is not superior to other languages. But it's my job to prepare my children for an opportunity to lead first-rate lives, and that opportunity increases if they have a fine command of English. We live in the United States, where command of English is *essential* to getting a good job.

I have an educational agenda.

Many people in the public schools want certain things done for economic or political reasons. Frequently, teachers attending staff development meetings are taught not by master teachers but by publishing-company employees. Why do fifth-grade teachers need hours of instruction before they can use a fifth-grade math book? Book publishers don't go to bed at night worrying that Johnny can't read; they worry about sales and profits. If our teachers can't teach, they're unlikely to be reformed by textbook publishers. My school currently has two literacy coaches—former teachers—who constantly beg me to use their materials with my children. When these coaches try to convince me about their approaches, they rarely rely on arguments about improving reading. At the end of the last school year, my fifth-graders scored in the ninety-first percentile in national tests while the rest of the school scored in the forties. The coaches know this, so why do they want me to change my methods? They want to satisfy their boss, who wants to please his boss, who wants to impress her boss—administrators all. It's insulting (and boring) to listen to them drone on about how to use their books. The same song-and-dance routine accompanies the promotion of the latest new-and-improved math textbook. Seriously, how many ways can you teach a child his multiplication tables? Arithmetic hasn't changed. If a math text is so complicated that the average fifth-grade teacher can't understand it without hours of instruction, then there's something wrong with the book, the teacher, or both. These companies interfere with creative and effective teachers. If we want Johnny to calculate better, we need to hire better teachers, not buy newer textbooks.

People with political agendas cause other kinds of problems. They want to legislate whose voices we hear in the classroom by banning books and ideas. In my class, any and all voices need to be included. When we learn about the Indian Wars, Chief Red Cloud gets equal time with General Sherman. In literature, Malcolm X gets equal time with Ayn Rand. Educators need to encourage critical thinking rather than promote indoctrination.

Several years ago I had a substitute teacher take my class for the day. Afterward he wrote me an angry note. While he loved my class and appreciated the easy-to-follow lesson plans I had left for him, he was incensed that I had a picture of Malcolm X hanging on the wall. We had been reading *The Autobiography of Malcolm X* (the sub refused to read it with them and instead had the students watch television during the scheduled reading hour). He did tell the kids that Malcolm X was a thug and that I, too, must be a thug if I was using that book in my class.

The next time he was assigned a class on our campus, the sub came to my room and started screaming at me. I calmed him down and tried to explain that I didn't agree with everything Malcolm X wrote. I told him that I felt Alex Haley and Malcolm X had written a fascinating book (my students would certainly agree) and that his voice, whether you agree with him or not, was an important one in American history. I told him that the students had lively and thoughtful discussions provoked by Malcolm X's words, and that they looked forward to watching Spike Lee's extraordinary film when they finished the book. When the substitute calmed down, he told me he admired me as a teacher but would pay me $100 to remove the picture.

He gave me the $100. I took the picture down and used the money to help buy copies of *The Catcher in the Rye*. Several months later, I had to miss a day of school and deliberately asked for him to be the substitute. When I returned the next day, another angry letter was waiting for me.

I don't know why he was angry. Malcolm X was gone. And the picture of Che Guevara looked really good in his place.

I will not waste time.

In the Los Angeles Unified School District we are allotted 163 days of instructional time with our students. That's fewer than thirty-three weeks, but even much of this precious time will be wasted. "Last days" of school before vacation are usually filled with parties and cleanup; days of return are similarly wasted setting up and adjusting. There are holidays and other interruptions, including, of course, the time wasted listening to the publishing companies explain the new textbooks. Even with my no-shortcut schedule, which keeps my students in school approximately three hundred days of the year, there is never enough time to help them soar to the highest of heights.

The system, in its never-ending quest to fix things, is constantly sending teachers off to meetings and classes that have absolutely no effect on the quality of education the children are receiving. I try to avoid these meetings by quietly backing out and continuing to work with the students.

It's not that I'm against meetings; I've gone to gatherings where I've met superb educators who have been instrumental in my success in the classroom. That's time well spent. However . . .

A few years ago, my district set up three days of specialized instruction to help teachers improve. All district schools were under fire because of our low test scores. My immediate supervisor, who knew of my reluctance to attend these sessions, cornered me and made me promise to be there. He mentioned my pay being withheld and posed other veiled threats if I didn't attend. I had planned, during those three days, to read *Animal Farm* with my students, take them to a college day at UCLA to attend the volleyball matches and have dinner, do an additional six hours of problem solving, and finish building and launching our rockets. Instead, I went to three days of meetings.

The first day was a seminar on how to use the new math books being distributed in our classrooms. I knew I was in trouble when, at the start of the session, we spent half an hour learning that since there were thirty-two chapters and thirty weeks of the school year, we should plan on doing about one chapter a week. I drove fifteen miles to learn this.

The math session was scheduled to last from 8:00 to 2:30. But by 11:30 the publishers had gone over everything they wanted to say (and this included a thirty-minute break). They told us to go to lunch and be back at 12:30. I asked why were we coming back if the session was over. They told me the district had dictated the times, and they had sign-up sheets and guards at the door to make sure all teachers returned. We did, and sat for two hours in silence until we were dismissed.

The following day I was sent to a session on using music in the classroom. This was a worthwhile experience for novice teachers. The problem was that the instructor was a good one who spent the entire day explaining how to read music and play about four notes on a recorder. As it happens, I am well versed in music instruction and have children playing six-part Bach pieces on classical guitars as part of a two-hour concert each year. Why was I here? I sat all day looking out the window at a beautiful bright blue sky with no wind—perfect for launching rockets.

The last day was the worst. We went to a computer lab to learn how to use the Internet. I know how to use the Internet but am certainly interested in learning more. However, the computer server was down, and none of the computers was working. The teachers simply sat at their terminals talking. I did not return after lunch.

Last year the same schedule of instruction was arranged. I attended no sessions, and my pay was indeed docked. My class, however, read Orwell, went to a David Hockney exhibit, learned to take photographs the way he does, and launched rockets amid laughter and marvel.

The following week I was called in and warned. This year they have added an additional two days of staff development, and I had better attend or there will be serious consequences. I didn't protest at all. I sat there nodding my head and thinking. Two additional days—that's enough time to fit in Maya Angelou.

CHAPTER 5

Running on Empty

ttention! I have an announcement to all the young teachers out there who are working very hard (and there are a lot of you). I've got some bad news. Just because you're working hard doesn't mean you're a good teacher. It just means you're working hard. I'm sorry if that sounds callous, but I know the symptoms, because I was the hardest-working young teacher anyone has ever seen. And I do not say that proudly. I'm about to paint a picture of a caring but foolish young man in the hope that my foolishness may help a few young teachers avoid the mistakes I made.

Don't get me wrong: I'm still working harder than practically anyone. But in my early years, only a lunatic or a drug addict could have kept my schedule, and I don't do drugs.

By my fourth year of teaching, I was:

Teaching my class of forty fifth-graders from 8:00 A.M. to 3:00 P.M., five days a week

Starting school at 6:30 A.M. for kids who wanted an extra ninety minutes of math

Giving up my recess and lunch to teach twenty kids to play guitar

Staying after school until 5:00 P.M. to produce a Shakespeare play with fifty kids

Working three nights a week from 5:30 P.M. until midnight

Working two nights a week from 11:00 P.M. until 5:00 A.M.

Working all weekends from 11:00 A.M. until 2:00 A.M. in the morning

Coming in every day of vacation to teach students from 6:00 A.M. to 5:00 P.M. (unpaid)

Raising enough money for all our extra supplies

Taking my class to Washington, D.C., for a week during the year

Taking my class to the Oregon and San Diego Shakespeare Festivals

Having read about some of our activities, you may have asked yourself a very important question: Where is he getting the money to buy guitars? He must be buying some of his literature books. How is he able to finance a Shakespeare production? Where do his Shakespeare texts come from? How do the kids get to Washington?

It's possible that you'll admire me for the tale I'm about to tell, but I assure you I'm not seeking your admiration here. I'm telling you this in the hope that you will not be as stupid (my wife uses the word "eccentric") as I was.

As I mentioned, the Jungle made me angry, and I was determined to do *something*. I knew that my class desperately needed all kinds of supplies that would cost thousands of dollars a year (the annual Shakespeare production alone costs over $5,000). I was constantly taking children to meals. I made sure every child received a birthday present. On Christmas Day, I would go to the home of every Christian child and leave a present at the door. I spent thousands on art supplies and sports equipment. The materials that were easy to get or were supplied by wealthy parents back at Camelot were nowhere to be found in the Jungle.

To come up with the needed money, I began to work extra jobs. I worked after school for a messenger service, driving all over the city with small packages. I delivered weekends for a delicatessen. I even spent one year working weekends for an ice-cream company, getting up Saturday and Sunday mornings at 5:00 A.M. to drive hundreds of miles to dozens of supermarkets, checking the arrangement of the merchandise in the freezer (before going to my deli job). Worse still, I used to usher for rock concerts, where my job was to stand in the men's room to make sure no trouble erupted. The only trouble was watching drugged-out fans vomit all over the place, and occasionally on me. That didn't bother me too much—the red usher jacket was ugly anyway. In my darkest of days, having finished work for a messenger service, I worked a graveyard shift all night long delivering newspapers. I'd catch a quick shower back home at 5:30 A.M. before heading to school. But despite all this, there was never enough money. Every time I was short taking the kids on a trip or buying equipment, I used credit cards until I was sinking in an ocean of plastic debt.

My classroom was well supplied, but the real expenses were the trips I was taking with the students. We began going to Washington, D.C., each year and really doing the town. Many school groups spent three or four days there, whereas our class was spending twelve. We spent several days a year at the San Diego Shakespeare Festival and a week at the Oregon Shakespeare Festival in Ashland. I was earning over $30,000 a year but spending even more just on classroom supplies and trips with the children.

These sacrifices may seem noble, but the truth is, I was all heart and no brains. You readers who are not teachers can have no idea how many teachers constantly reach into their own pockets for classroom supplies. I was an extreme example, but believe me, every good teacher out there spends far too much of his or her own money. It would be nice if teachers were given a realistic budget for the extra art supplies, science materials, sports equipment, and books they buy for their classes on a regular basis.

My debts mounted. My credit cards were so far over the limit, I was afraid to open my mailbox or answer the phone. I was so determined to save the world, I couldn't see what was happening to me. My health was deteriorating rapidly, and my wife-to-be was really concerned. If I got four hours of sleep, I considered it a good night.

It got worse. During my fourth year of teaching, my car died and I had no money for another one. The mechanic told me the old one was not worth fixing, so I sold it for scrap and worked out a schedule by which I would take the bus to and from work. I lived about thirty miles from the Jungle and had to be up by 3:15 A.M. to catch the three buses it would take to get me to the classroom by 6:00. Without a car, I was unable to work my other jobs, so I had less money than before. By this point I was like an animal. Logical thought was rarely a part of my daily routine. The kids were worried about me. Several would walk me to the bus stop at 6:00 P.M., and if I caught the buses just right, I might be home by nine. I was often trying to get by with two or three hours of sleep.

I had no idea how much strain the bus rides were going to be. I was jammed into a mass of humanity for hours at a time. Several times on the ride home at night, people threw up on me. My favorite memory is of sitting between two guys who were discussing how easy it was for them to get out of jail. One told the other, "They could never pin that murder on me." Lovely!

Friday nights were the worst. I'd get back to my apartment building and climb the stairs. Often I would wake up Saturday mornings on the floor of my living room facedown on the carpet with my clothes and backpack still on. The scariest part was that I wouldn't remember coming into the house. By Saturday morning, I was coherent enough to begin planning for the week ahead and grading all the papers left over from the previous few days. I'd rush through the papers before catching the bus to my deli job. Barbara noticed that on my worst days, my skin actually had a greenish tint.

Looking back, I see that all my good intentions were more than just foolish—I wasn't accomplishing nearly as much in the classroom as I imagined. I would have been a better teacher without my quixotic dreams. There were days when my exhaustion turned me into an ogre. Remember the scene in *It's a Wonderful Life* when George Bailey frightens his children by yelling at them when he thinks his life is ruined? I've played that scene. There were too many days when I snapped at children but I should have been compassionate and understanding. But I was so worn out. Saving the world is not an easy job.

It's embarrassing to realize that one has been a complete

idiot. Time after time there were warning signs—that's not accurate, *fireworks exploding, flashing neon warning signs*—that I didn't notice. I was without perspective because practically every ounce of my energy was going into my classroom. When I married Barbara, I added four step-children to my list of responsibilities. They were stepchildren from God, because, like their mother, they put up with my devotion to my students.

One year I had an outstanding class of both fifth- and sixth-graders. I had saved enough money from various jobs to take them on a camping trip at the end of the year. Our school was on its year-round schedule, and our last day was April 30. This class and I would be on vacation in May, and my new class would begin in June.

I looked at the calendar and counted my students. I had thirty of them equally divided between the fifth and sixth grades, so I decided to take two separate trips with the kids. Both groups would get to camp in Yosemite and Sequoia National Parks and finish their trips with whitewater river rafting. The fifth-graders would take slightly easier hikes and go rafting through the Gold Country on the American River below Sacramento. They would come back on a Friday night after their two weeks. This would allow me to teach my former students on Saturday morning before leaving that afternoon with the sixth-grade students. The sixth-grade trip would feature more difficult hikes and run the rougher waters of the Merced River below Yosemite. (I know—I should have been locked up.)

After the trips were planned and nonrefundable fees paid to various campgrounds and rafting companies, I received the extraordinary news that Miep Gies would be able to visit my class. Miep is the amazing heroine who protected

Anne Frank's family for over two years and found the diary. It was Miep who saved Anne's words for the world and nursed Anne's father, Otto, back to health when he returned from the concentration camps. My classes had written to her for years, and now she was paying us a visit. For a teacher, it does not get any better than that. My students, both present and past, were thrilled beyond words.

She was going to visit on the Saturday morning between the two trips. This meant more work for me, as we invited all sorts of people and prepared special songs and presents for her. Since we were getting back at about ten on Friday evening, I figured I would have time that night to accomplish these things.

I was then notified that a local group of schools was interested in having me speak to them about teaching on that same Saturday afternoon. They were paying the substantial sum of $200, and I desperately needed the money to help finance the trips. My own children were already in college, and our bills were really mounting. I told the group yes, I would speak.

The first camping trip went well. But as we were returning on Friday night, a big accident on the freeway into Los Angeles caused delays, and we didn't get back until four in the morning. I was in class by five to prepare for Miep, who was showing up at eight. Two hundred students would be there as well. She arrived and gave an inspiring talk that affected the life of everyone there.

By eleven that morning I was racing crosstown to give the speech. I did an adequate job and received a more than adequate paycheck. I felt tired but good returning to school at two, where the fifteen sixth-graders were eagerly waiting. We'd be in Sequoia that night.

Six hours later, with the sun setting beautifully over the chillier than usual mountains at our campsite among the California redwoods, I told my students that I was exhausted. After a quick dinner I begged them to let me get a night's sleep, promising that the real fun would begin tomorrow. The kids were understanding and told me they'd hit the sack and leave me alone for a night. There would be plenty of other nights for campfires, singing, and ghost stories.

Of course, as my head hit the soft spot on my sleeping bag, I heard one of the kids cry out excitedly, "Look, it's snowing!" Within fifteen minutes we were in a blizzard. Somehow we managed to pack, load up, and find our way to a local hotel in the national park. We spent ten fun-filled days playing in the snow, but I was the least prepared of everyone on the trip. When we returned, my students graduated and started a three-month vacation. I was beginning my new class the next day. I was exhausted and seriously ill, sneezing, coughing, and vomiting for much of the next two months. Needless to say, the new class got off to a terrible start. Eventually they had a good year, yet I wonder how much better they would have been with a healthy and energetic leader. My enormous overexertion was actually preventing me from achieving what I was hoping to accomplish. Yet two years later, matters grew even worse. It seems ridiculous, looking back, but when one is in the middle of a hurricane, it's hard to find fair winds. Barbara was begging me to take it easy, but in those days I wouldn't have taken notice of a burning bush.

Things finally came to a head on another camping trip. I had always done a thorough job planning such outings: the itinerary was always organized, and the kids had a great time and were well cared for.

Barbara, a registered nurse, had begun coming on the trips, and we were a fine team. However, just before a camping trip to Yosemite, she became ill with a heart problem, and I had to lead the group of fifteen fifth-graders alone. Still, I wasn't concerned; we were staying in AAA-approved campgrounds with plenty of adult campers and rangers nearby to help out if problems arose, and by now I was an experienced leader of such excursions.

We camped in Yosemite National Park for several days, then headed for the coast and Monterey. Outside of San Francisco one night, I started having a severe allergic reaction. My eyes were swollen shut and I could barely breathe. I tried to fight it for several days, thinking I was just run-down. The kids were afraid for me, but I kept telling them I could weather the storm. Finally late one night I couldn't get any air at all and began vomiting blood. I gasped out a few instructions. They were to take my credit cards and stay in their tents while I tried to get myself to a hospital. If I wasn't back by morning, they were to go to the campground ranger; he was to call Barbara and she would help them get home. Somehow I made it to the campground ranger, who was happy to keep an eye on the kids. Years later, these kids told me they spent the evening outside their tents watching the night sky and praying over shooting stars that I wouldn't die.

In some of life's scariest moments, there is still humor. As I drove crazily down the night highway eight miles to the hospital, I began vomiting more blood. I was covered in it and terrified I would pass out at the wheel. I tried to calm myself by turning on the radio. The Beatles were singing "I Feel Fine." Bravo for life's little ironies!

I made it through the emergency doors and collapsed

on the floor. I was put on the table and the personnel explained to me that I was having an asthma attack. They helped open my bronchial tubes, and by four in the morning I was breathing steadily again. They wanted me to stay there for twenty-four-hour observation; a doctor promised to return after I had slept for a few hours. I sneaked out of the room by climbing through the window and made it back to the campground. I was pretty shaky, but we finished the five days we had left of the camping trip.

Barbara was furious when I got home. She taught me a lesson, which is the point of this story. "Rafe," she told me, "think of getting on an airplane. They always tell you that if oxygen masks come down, put your own on before assisting the child next to you."

She was right. I wasn't going to do anybody any good if I ruined my health. Only by taking care of myself would I ever be able to properly take care of others. It was time to start thinking about becoming an adult.

The reality is that many teachers push themselves to extraordinary limits because they care so much and it's very difficult to help children to a significantly better future. After all these years, I still push myself hard, but I've gained enough self-control to move from the insanity ward to the merely eccentric. Clearly, I haven't yet found the balance a wise and successful teacher should have, but I no longer buy presents for the kids—they are not part of an educational agenda—and if I choose to push myself hard, I make sure it's for a good purpose.

This past year my school schedule gave me the month of June off, and again I hoped to travel with two deserving groups of students. Here is evidence that one can still work extremely hard but, with a little wisdom and experience, achieve a better result.

My class of fifth-graders had graduated from elementary school, and as I now do every other year, I took them on what we call a Western Adventure. The kids study the Indian Wars of the post–Civil War era and even read Dee Brown's epic *Bury My Heart at Wounded Knee*. Forty-four students traveled with me on our private bus for fourteen days across South Dakota, Montana, and Wyoming to gain an understanding of Native American history. A highlight of the trip was a visit to Red Cloud's grave at Oglala, South Dakota, where we were fortunate enough to meet Tae Red Cloud, the chief's great-great-great-great-great granddaughter. From Mount Rushmore to hiking deep into the Grand Tetons, it was an adventure none of these children will ever forget.

When we flew home from Salt Lake City, a very special group of thirteen high school students was waiting for me. These were former students who had been preparing for college by working tremendously hard on Saturday mornings for the past four years. They were now finishing ninth and tenth grades and were going to visit twenty-five of the nation's finest universities with me. All of these students had high test scores and, more important, outstanding character. They had earned such a trip because going to schools like Princeton or Northwestern was no longer just a dream for them—admission had become a real possibility.

I was on the road for thirty-one straight days with these students and came home exhausted. The first group I had taken was waiting for me. They had rehearsed all year long to prepare a spectacular concert, had been resting for two weeks, and couldn't wait to get started with final preparations. These kids had as good a rock-and-roll band as any class of mine had ever produced, and they were fired up and ready to go. Of course, they hadn't practiced in over a month and desperately wanted to play. Our scheduled concert was in nine days.

But I was tired and told them so. I took a week off. Barbara and I went away and pampered ourselves. Phones were turned off, lesson plans were left behind, and we read junk and wasted our time doing things too frivolous to mention, in a town where we learned nothing and did nothing to better the fate of the world.

When I returned, the kids were in a panic, but I was relaxed and happy. The concert was in two days, and we had two days of excellent rehearsals. When the curtain finally went up and the kids opened with a blistering rendition of Sting's "Roxanne," the audience went wild. The entire night had a fresh and absolutely electric excitement. The kids never sounded better. It was easily the best concert a class of mine had ever given.

To all of you who are proud that you put your students first, make sure you give yourself equal time. It's rather romantic to say you'd die for your students. I used to say that. I now know I'm worth more to them alive.

CHAPTER 6

The Heart of the Matter

E very teacher has his share of disappointments, hurt, and even pain. If you care a lot, all of those aches are magnified. This chapter is about the worst time of my teaching life.

I had always been able to deal with most of the expected frustrations that come with teaching. I'd actually gotten used to, and even expected, obstacles to be placed in my way by an apathetic community, an out-of-control bureaucracy, impoverished families, and mediocre colleagues. I was not, however, able to handle the utter and complete pain I received at the hands of some of my favorite students.

I thought I understood and would be able to handle the anguish that a child can dispense. I had received wounds over the years that were painful but not mortal. I'll use Ann as an example. Ann was one of the brightest students I've ever had in my class. She was outstanding in everything. In fifth grade she was already reading at a high school level. She absorbed any piece of literature I placed in front of her. She completed first-year algebra with me. She was a brilliant writer, an accomplished artist, and a superior musician. She was a hungry and diligent student who would settle for nothing less than perfection.

Her mother had the same fire and conferred with me often to make sure her daughter would have a chance to be admitted to a private school in Los Angeles. I assured her mother I would do all the necessary work with Ann to get her accepted, and spent many extra hours tutoring her with standardized tests to ready her for the entrance exams, and prepared her for interviews as well. Ann got in easily and was soon the leading student at a prestigious academy. She wrote me many letters and often stopped by the classroom to thank me for having helped her. I, of course, told her the truth: the teacher opens the door, but it's the student who walks through. It was nice, though, being appreciated.

Tragedy struck a couple of years later. Ann's parents owned a small store, and her father was shot in the neck during a robbery. My brother is an important administrator in a fine hospital. We made sure the father went there and that he received excellent medical care. He made a full recovery.

Meanwhile, I helped the family by working for two months at their store. I would go there every day after school and help take care of things, including making Ann and her mother feel safe. People thought I was crazy spending so much time there, but I was glad to do it because Ann was such a special student.

When Ann's father went back to work, I was no longer

needed at the store. I never received any thank-you from the family for my time and efforts, which bothered me a bit, but they had been through a lot, and it was understandable.

I didn't hear from Ann for two years after this period. Then one day she called me because she had an opportunity to go east and attend a summer session for high school students at an Ivy League college. I helped her buy a plane ticket and wrote to her several times that summer but received no answer.

Three more years passed, and then her mother showed up at school one day. She wanted to tell me that Ann had been accepted into one of the world's most famous universities.

Yet Ann had never returned to school to watch our Shakespeare productions, as so many other alumni had done. She had never come back and spoken to my current classes about how they, too, could aim high and succeed. Still, I was happy that she had made it to the big time. For a student from the Jungle, that was quite a feat.

I have never heard from her since. I have to admit that this disturbed me, but some students express appreciation for a teacher's extra efforts and others do not. After all, no child can ever give to a teacher or parent the same support and caring he or she received from the adult. It's not supposed to be a two-way street. As I say, it's nice to be appreciated, but I knew that a good teacher finds satisfaction in good work done, and if a child expresses gratitude, that's just icing on the cake. I was disappointed that I never heard from Ann again, but I never lost any sleep over it.

What followed did not disturb my sleep—it murdered it.

There are students who cause much more consternation than an ungrateful youngster. These are the students who go on to middle school only to fall victim to the pressures of adolescence. It always hurts me to hear that a terrific kid with lots of brains and talent has joined a gang or begun drinking in the seventh or eighth grade. I spend long hours trying to figure out what I've done wrong or how I could have prevented such a thing from happening. Perhaps I had created a classroom where things were too pleasant and some of the kids weren't strong enough to handle the "real world" of schools, where dance steps and outfits mean more than algebra and literature. Perhaps I had made school so challenging and exciting that the boredom many of my former students found waiting in middle school led them to seek excitement elsewhere. Whatever the causes, I still am able to balance the occasional disappointing news of a troubled child with the many success stories I receive from a continuous stream of returning students who stop by to stay in touch.

But the Musketeers proved to be something different.

Some years ago, I had a particularly brilliant group of students. They were not only high achievers but also hard workers. They bonded well as a team. Each day was exciting. I felt I was coming into my own as a teacher. Not a day went by when I didn't go home feeling terrific. I was married to a fabulous woman, work was joyous, and I didn't even guess that this combination would one day help lead me to win a national teaching award. I had the greatest class of kids ever, or so I thought. I figured things could not get better.

Well, first of all, they could get better (and have).

And second of all, they could get a helluva lot worse (and did).

There were many memorable kids in this class, but three girls were special to me. They had all come from homes with fairly severe problems. They weren't Cosby kids, believe me.

The three girls hit it off with one another and, in turn, hit it off with me. They became my advisers for almost any issue that affected the class. We spent hundreds of extra hours together. I constantly sang their praises to my family. More than any other children I had met up to this time, these three showed me the unlimited potential of young people when challenged to reach for the stars. They excelled in every subject, and being their teacher was a pleasure.

And they were inseparable. They called themselves the Musketeers, even though we had never read Dumas' book. Looking back, it's almost unimaginable what these children got to do. Our class went to Washington that year, along with an endless series of concerts, sporting events, and exciting activities.

When this class graduated from elementary school, they made a suggestion: they wanted me to teach a Saturday class for my former students. They were bored in middle school and wanted a challenge, so I created a Saturday morning program in which sixth- and seventh-graders could study Shakespeare and begin preparing for standardized tests like the SAT. The reward for all the extra study would be a trip to the Oregon Shakespeare Festival in Ashland the following summer.

This first year went well, I thought, and my wife and daughter came with us to Ashland. However, they weren't as impressed with the Musketeers as I was. Don't get me wrong: they liked the students and found them to be very bright. They just didn't believe these kids were particularly special. I thought my family didn't know the kids as well as I did. Talk about blind! I might as well have been King Lear.

The serious trouble began after the trip to Ashland.

September came, and we started a new year of Saturday classes for former students. One girl who had done very well decided not to attend. I thought I had been close to this child, who was a very sweet kid with a delightfully eccentric personality. I heard the kids gossiping about her. They said she had begun hanging around the wrong crowd. I was shocked and responded with the stupidest action a teacher can make: I got involved in discussing her with her peers.

It wasn't done out of malice, and it wasn't anger or disappointment. It was fear and concern. I wanted to know what was going on and if there was anything I could do to help this kid stay on the right path.

However, good intentions count for absolutely nothing when a child's feelings are on the line. This was a child who needed support, understanding, compassion, and a firm but loving leader who would be there for her always. She didn't need a frustrated "after all we've learned" lecture from an adult who violated her privacy by talking about her with her peers. Word got back to her about the discussion, and of course the word that got back had been modified by so many go-betweens that she received a message of pure rejection, scorn, and disapproval.

I took a bad situation and made it worse. Any good parent or teacher will tell you that on many occasions kids need space. They need to figure things out for themselves. I hadn't understood this and was constantly interfering with the kids' attempts to branch out and develop. It was Roy Hobbs all over again. I may have recognized in my head that I didn't want to be him, but I still wasn't really seeing things from the child's point of view. If a kid didn't want to participate in my program, I should have supported that decision. Foolishly, if a child walked out the door, I followed and tried to persuade him or her to return. At this point someone should have shouted at me about horses and water, but clearly I wasn't thinking or listening.

I still couldn't see the storm coming. I was unable to understand that this girl's problems weren't unique but a symptom of much that was wrong with my teaching strategies.

As the months wore on, it was clear to me that the majority of my former students felt being in such an unusual class had been a great experience. But other students were angry with me. One day, a fifth-grader came up and told me a curious story. She asked me if I knew a boy named Sean. I knew him well. Sean had been in my class four years before and an excellent student. He had been on trips and had lots of friends. He was a baseball junkie. My wife and I took his class to their first baseball game and bought him his first glove.

The fifth-grader told me she had been walking down the street wearing her Shakespearean T-shirt that kids in my class often wore. Sean walked up to her and asked her if she was in my class. She happily said she was.

Sean said, "Be sure to tell Mr. Esquith 'Fuck you.' "

I had no idea where this came from—not a clue. It hurt enormously but puzzled me even more than it hurt. My entire family put their heads together and couldn't figure it out. We had always been good to Sean.

The Musketeers were not coming around to visit as often as they once had. This was to be expected, as they were getting older and their schedules were so busy. It was troubling, though, that when they did visit, they were rather nasty in their conversations with me. I tried to see this as a symptom of adolescent rebellion, but there was something meaner than teenage moodiness in most of these encounters. There was anger and even hatred.

I was upset that some children were making what I felt were poor decisions, and there was nothing wrong with that. My huge mistake was to indulge my own pain when I hadn't been sensitive or wise enough to feel *their* frustrations. They were angry with me for butting in to their affairs. We had spent so much time together that I thought this gave me the right to tell them all that was right or wrong with the world. It's easy to fall into that trap; as adults, we often see things children do not. The hard part is to let go and allow the child take what you have taught and go off on his own journey. I wasn't a wise enough person to let that happen.

As a result, there were kids who had once loved being in my class but had come to be angry with me personally. They knew they had learned many good things, and were glad that they had, but they also sensed my disapproval of parts of their lives that were clearly none of my business. They knew my opinions of fashion, television shows, music, and politics. There was nothing wrong with this, but I had never made it clear that they could disagree with me about any and all of these things and still be considered terrific kids. They desperately wanted my approval and became furious with me when they felt that the price they had to pay was to follow my advice and guidance in all areas of life. What a fool I was!

It started to get to me. My current class was going well, but the kids would often come up and say things to me like "Are you okay, Mr. Esquith?" I had always tried to leave any personal problems or pain outside the class; I figured the kids had enough problems of their own without my adding to them. For the first time, I was unable to put on a mask of optimism for the children. I was too frustrated. If kids whom I had given everything could be so angry with me, what was the point of ever doing anything for anyone?

The nadir of my teaching life came next. Among the many things I heard kids talking about was the trashing I was receiving at the hands (and mouths!) of the Musketeers. These were the same three girls who had once sent me beautiful letters and cards telling me what the class and I had meant to them. I would look at their old letters and hear of their ugly talk and get completely depressed.

One day I got a note at school from one of them, requesting that I write her a recommendation to enter a special magnet program. I wrote her an immature and nasty note in return, refusing her request. I told her my arm and shoulder were too sore to write a letter for her—they were strained from the knives I had been trying to pull out of my back.

The following Saturday I returned home from teaching in the morning to find a reply from her. To this day I have never read anything as angry and malicious as her letter. She attacked practically everything about my class, my family, and of course me. She told me I was a racist, favoring certain groups of students over others. She even made a list of students who despised my class and never had the courage to tell me. They hated the high standards; they hated having to work harder than other students; they hated that their parents loved my efforts. It was hard for me to read the whole letter the first time because my hands were shaking so badly.

I have a small study at home. I went in, sat down on the carpet with my back against the wall, and cried for hours. I didn't make any noise or move—I just sat there with the tears running down my face.

It was King Lear who commented, "How sharper than a serpent's tooth it is to have a thankless child," but I never really understood that line until I read the letter. I wasn't even angry; I was simply dead with pain. If I hadn't had a wife and family, I don't know what I might have done that night.

If I had been even slightly perceptive, I would have stopped feeling sorry for myself and thought about the pain some of these students were in. Today I would write a different letter. I would tell the little girl that I felt bad that things weren't good between us. I would tell her what a great kid she was and how lucky a teacher I was to have had her in the class. I would invite her to come on in so we could talk and work out any differences we had. It's easy to do this when you can see beyond yourself, but I hadn't come that far yet. How ironic that I loved George Harrison's song "Within You Without You." How many times had I sung "When you've seen beyond yourself, you may find peace of mind is waiting there" with absolutely no understanding?

The next few weeks were a blur. I taught every day, but I can't remember what we did in class, which is extremely unusual for me. I am a teacher who can tell you what he did with his students on the third Monday in March two years ago. But those weeks have disappeared from my mind.

One thing that kept me going were letters I received from other students who had heard I was in trouble. Many wrote me that they heard what had happened and not to let it get me down. Another wrote that she cried when she heard about what the letter said. She couldn't believe that her friends had simply "lost their minds." That helped a little, but not much.

Believe me, I'm a reasonably smart fellow, but I just

couldn't figure it out. What had happened? I tried to think back to every moment we had spent together. Had I said something harmful to these children? Had my expectations been too high? Was I just much meaner than I had thought I was? And, I reasoned, if I had made mistakes with these children, didn't the hundreds of times I went miles beyond the line of duty count for *something*?

I wasn't getting any closer to a solution as time passed. I couldn't sleep and had stopped being a good teacher. I had a very bright class filled with kind and hardworking children. Every day, my box at school was full of messages and letters congratulating me on being Disney's Outstanding Teacher of the Year. People kept telling me how lucky I was and how happy they were for me. They kept telling me no one deserved the honor more than I.

That made things worse. God, it hurt. As a child I lost my father and his memory haunts me. My mother died just before I became a teacher. I'd lost family and important friends in my life, but nothing hurt more than this. I didn't think I could ever recover.

I love math, but things just didn't add up for me. I now know how parents feel who sacrifice everything and still feel they fail. All that sacrifice—years of going without sleep— and a few students I had done so much for had absolutely crushed me. For the first time, I really felt this wasn't worth it.

And then Sheila came to the rescue. One day the kids were out having lunch and I was preparing a guitar lesson while I brooded in the classroom. I guess I looked pretty unhappy, because the first child who came back to class—a quiet girl who rarely drew attention to herself—walked over to me and said, "Are you okay, Mr. Esquith?"

I told her I was, which was a stupid thing to say. As any

teacher knows, lying to a bright fifth-grader is impossible. They always know the score.

I thought I had done a reasonable job of hiding my pain from the class. They knew I was a little down but had no concept that I was ready to give up completely. Sheila then began the longest conversation we ever had.

Sheila: Why don't you say what you're thinking? You always tell me I can talk to you about my problems. Why can't you?

Rafe: It's no big deal.

Sheila: It's about those girls, right?

Rafe: Yes, it is. I just can't believe the way they've acted. I can't believe they hate me so much.

Sheila: I can.

Rafe: What?

Sheila: I believe it. You don't know them, Mr. Esquith.

Rafe: What do you mean I don't know them?

Sheila: You don't know them. I've known them since I was in kindergarten. I've known them much longer than you have. They're not nice kids. You just don't see things.

Rafe: I've known them for almost three years.

Sheila: You only know them when they're around you. Lots of kids use you, Mr. Esquith. You just don't see it. You love them so much you don't see them clearly. You don't even know who some of your best students are.

My head was spinning. Was this possible?

It didn't happen immediately, but Sheila's remarks really got me thinking. I talked with my wife and she agreed. The easy route would be to dismiss these angry kids as adolescent cretins who weren't worth a cup of warm spit. But that would have been a lie. *I was to blame for these problems.* Many students were leaving my class and accomplishing things using my lessons and guidance. But some were leaving with bitter feelings, and if I wanted to change the situation, then I would have to change.

I wrote earlier that good teachers and parents stand for something. I wrote that there are some issues on which I won't back down. I still won't. However, there are times when a teacher or parent needs to *back up.*

I realized that the students who were the most upset with me had been the best students of all. Seeing their potential had made me turn up the pressure on them because I recognized just how far they could go. However, in my excitement, rather than show these kids various possible paths, I had shoved them down a particular road and not even given them a chance to consider other directions.

I needed to take a good look at my classroom through the eyes of the kids. I spent several evenings having dinner with some of my former students; I spoke very little and listened a lot. I learned quite a bit from them. It was a real education.

They taught me not to confuse academic excellence with character. When I came to the Jungle, I was shocked and upset by the incredibly low academic achievement of the students there. Over the first few years I was so determined to inspire students to achieve academic excellence that I was confusing my best *students* with my best *people*.

There were many students in my class who were doing very well in school to whom I hadn't given proper credit because they were overshadowed by my highest achievers. I needed to redefine in my mind what made a successful student.

Don't misunderstand me: I still have great expectations and try to inspire my students to reach the highest levels of scholarship. I have simply added to the list. Now I'm focusing on students who strive to reach the highest levels of humanity, which means that I'd better reach those levels as well.

How can you really know your kids? We all know that children will often act a certain way around adults to gain approval or reward. It's the kids themselves who really know one another, particularly in the area of character.

I once knew a well-respected teacher who was "shocked" when one of her students was caught shoplifting. The other kids in her class were quietly talking to one another at recess and I overheard them. They weren't surprised at all. They knew this kid.

I have learned that before I decide if a kid is truly special, I had better observe and listen to his peers. They are a much better judge of a child's worth and potential than I. They are the ones who know if the child is nice to play with, easy to get along with, and honest and decent. As teachers or parents, we have a very limited view. Yes, we have a lot to say, but so do our children.

With better vision, we sacrifice for students for whom that sacrifice will most likely pay off. I'm sorry to say this, but there are times when even superhuman effort will not save a child from his environment or himself. It's not the job of the teacher to save a child's soul; it is the teacher's job to provide an opportunity for the child to save his own soul.

One of the biggest mistakes I was making was a matter of style. As an adult, I often felt I knew "what was best" for a student. I used to insist students come early for math team or stay late for Shakespeare. Yes, it's good for the children to do those things, but they need to feel that they have the option not to do them and not feel guilty. I had set up a classroom climate in which students felt they had to accomplish things to please me. I had underestimated how much my approval meant to them.

My ex-students and I went over the angry letter I had received. They showed me something interesting—the word "worship" was written over and over again. Any student who became angry with me had at one time "worshiped" me. The kids explained to me that my approval was so important that students who felt I disapproved of them were devastated. That devastation turned to anger. I needed to improve my teaching by offering just as many opportunities for students while supporting them in whatever paths they chose, even if I knew the paths to be wrong. That was for the students to find out.

It was astonishing how much I learned listening to these former students. They were some of my toughest critics and, at the same time, my best friends in the world. They advised me well. But I was still feeling very low; absorbing all the things the kids were teaching me was going to take time.

I realized then that when a person goes through a terrible experience, one of three things can happen. He can become embittered by it and be angry; can be defeated by it and be depressed; or can learn from it and grow. Growing from pain is definitely the hardest route to follow, and it is the one I chose.

I decided to apply my new lessons. I would keep my standards high but sharpen my vision and my hearing in evaluating my students. I needed to improve my communication with the kids. They had to understand that they would never "let me down" no matter what they had done wrong. They needed to know that I would still be the toughest teacher they ever had. They also had to learn that I was the nicest and most understanding one as well. They had to see I was placing the same demands on myself that I was placing on them. Every moment of every day had to involve an activity that combined a great time, the quest for academic excellence, and, most important of all, the building of character.

I wasn't yet sure how to accomplish all this, but I was finally asking the right questions. My answer was closer than I thought. It would come one night when my wife leaned over in bed and told me it was time to reread a certain book. But that was still a few weeks away.

I am no longer saddened by the Musketeers. If I had them in my class today our problems never would have occurred. I would have recognized them for their strengths and weaknesses and consequently not been disappointed with their actions. I also wouldn't have done so much for them, because I would have spent more time with other students for whom going the extra mile would be more effective.

Coming to understand all this was painful and difficult, but the challenge to me was clear. Huck Finn was gone, and Roy Hobbs had caused enough trouble. The search was on for someone who could show me the way. It was time to become the best teacher I could be.

And the Musketeers? One of them has dropped out of sight, while the others made it to good universities and live normal lives.

And Sheila, who saw it all? Sheila, who, unknown to me, was my best student that year? Sheila, who had average test scores and a very quiet voice? She went to an Ivy League school and has grown up to be a brilliant and beautiful woman. She married a terrific guy and has a fabulous career.

She is a teacher.

CHAPTER 7

On the Road to Find Out

After nine years in the classroom filled with many successes and just as many mistakes, I was still standing. The Musketeers had really injured me, and I was in a bad place. Yes, I knew that the most important thing in teaching and parenting (and life) is to know who you are. I just hadn't found the answer. And let me make it clear that the answer for me is certainly not going to be the right answer for you. I just knew that I could never be a good teacher without defining myself—a sort of personal mission statement.

I thought I was there. In my first few years of teaching, the one thing I could count on was teaching literature to children. As previously mentioned, I taught books that meant something to me, and I began to love one book more than the others. In doing so, I began to relate to one character more than any other. For several years this book and character became the highlight of my year of reading great novels with the students. It was Mark Twain's masterpiece, *The Adventures of Huckleberry Finn.*

God, did I love Huck. I still do. He is such a good person. He constantly makes the sound moral choice even though he believes himself to be evil. I loved Twain's brilliant use of irony. Most of all, I loved Jim and Huck's journey down the river. Two lost souls on the highway of life, to quote *Damn Yankees.* And most of all, I loved the end of the book.

In case you've forgotten, Huck and Jim both run away from society. It's a society filled with violence and racism and hypocrisy and dishonesty and meanness. Yet these two outcasts use their wits and love for each other to escape one predicament after another. And at the end of this long journey, Huck is given a chance to return to civilization. He has a chance to be raised "properly" and do things the way society wants him to.

And Huck, God bless him, rejects society. He's been there before. He decides to take Jim and Tom Sawyer and light out for the territory. Good for you, Huck! You tell them! Tell all those awful people to go **** themselves.

I believed that Huck had replaced Roy Hobbs as my role model. I, too, would reject society, and a school system damaged beyond repair. If a few cool kids wanted to light out for the territory with me, they were welcome to come aboard the raft on which I sailed.

Except I had come to a point where no one was getting on board the raft with me. I loved Huck, but I was still lost. I thought I knew who I was, but to be Huck was not to be a great teacher.

It took a ten-year-old to challenge and humble me into

seeing that Huck was not the answer for me. It was the first day of my new class. The Musketeers were gone but my nerves were exposed and raw. I was in no mood to be a good teacher. I just knew that no kid was ever going to use and abuse me the way those three ingrates had. It was easier being mad at them than being mad at myself.

As my students entered the first day, a tiny little girl with bangs came up to me. In a bag she had some breakfast food purchased at a fast-food store, and she told me she had bought me breakfast for our first day together.

"What's your name?" I asked her.

"Joann," she said quietly.

"Well, listen then, Joann," I said. "You don't have to buy me breakfast or kiss up to me. If you want to be successful in this class, just do your best and we'll get along just fine—but no presents—got it?"

"Yes," she said and found a seat.

The first week went by smoothly. On Friday, I gathered the students in what we call a Magic Circle. The students sit in a circle and share their feelings about any and all issues, ranging from school subjects to family problems.

"Well," I told them proudly, "I think we've had a good first week. Our reading and math have been excellent, and everyone is doing a fine job. Does anyone have anything to say about this week we've spent together?"

For the first time since Monday, Joann raised her hand. "I have something to say, Rafe," she began. "You know, last Monday, when I brought you breakfast, I wasn't trying to kiss up to you. You really don't understand." She went on softly but with the determination and confidence of someone speaking the truth from the heart. "I've been waiting my whole life to be in your class. Ever since I was a first-grader, I've watched your class. You always have the coolest things. You have the best kids. You have great plays and play the best music. Your kids have the most fun. My parents think you're a god. They've seen you on television and read about you in newspapers and magazines."

Man, the room was quiet. This little girl was on a roll.

"I wasn't trying to kiss up to you. I was just so happy to be here that I wanted to tell you that. I wanted to tell you how happy I was that I was going to have you for my teacher. *And you really hurt my feelings. I wanted you to know that you really hurt me.*"

I was devastated. This little girl spoke so simply and honestly that there was only one thing I could do. To borrow from Holden Caulfield, I apologized like a madman. I promised her that if she ever gave me another chance, I would never treat her like that again.

Battered and bruised but not defeated, I began work with this new class. One night, as I've said, my wife suggested to me that it was time to reread a particular book. It was a book I had read twice before and loved both times. Yet I hadn't really understood it. I was now ready to find the role model who had the answer for me. I reread Harper Lee's *To Kill a Mockingbird,* and I realized I had found my hero in Atticus Finch.

I had thought this novel was about a trial. It is, of course, but it's about much more than that. Early in the story, Atticus returns home to find his little daughter, Scout, crying. She has been brutally teased at school and asks her father, "Atticus, do you defend niggers?"

When Atticus corrects her racist remark, Scout merely

explains that it's not her word but what the children are saying at school. She can't understand why Atticus is defending someone when the whole town doesn't think he should. Why is he doing this?

"For a number of reasons," Atticus replies. The most important one, he explains, is that if he didn't, he could never tell his children what to do anymore. He could not hold his head up in front of them.

Atticus's son, Jem, asks his father if they're going to win the case, and Atticus replies quietly, "No."

It hit me like a thunderbolt. You see, Atticus knows everything Huck knows. He knows society is racist. He recognizes the violence, hypocrisy, injustice, and ignorance of society. He knows he is going to lose.

But Atticus does not light out for the territory. He goes into the courtroom to fight the fight as best as he can, because it is what he believes in. He doesn't do it because of the law, or the rules, or what people will think. He has his own code, and he lives by it as well as he can.

I still cry when I think about this. My classroom is my courtroom. I am going to lose more than I win. There are many times when, despite my efforts, I will lose children to poverty, ignorance, and, most tragically, a society that embraces mediocrity.

But that doesn't paralyze me anymore. I have a code, as any good teacher or parent must have. It doesn't matter if I lost a battle yesterday. It doesn't matter if the odds are against me. It doesn't matter if I'm just one fellow trying to fight television, corporations, and a society that hasn't yet achieved Dr. Martin Luther King's dream of judging someone by the content of his character.

I knew that I had to be the person I wanted the kids to be. I never want my kids to be depressed or despairing about any bad breaks or failures that they've had. Well, that had to apply to me as well. I now knew that if I wanted the kids to work hard, then I'd better be the hardest-working person they'd ever known. If I wanted them to be kind, I'd better be the kindest human being they'd ever met. Teaching must be by example, not by lecture.

I've made plenty of mistakes since rediscovering Atticus, but I've always been able to hold my head up to my students. Atticus showed me the way.

I had come to the same understanding that Jem reached. As a little boy, Jem never understood his father's greatness. Midway through the novel, as he comes to appreciate his father's intelligence, courage, and humility, he runs down the street and calls out, "Atticus is a gentleman, just like me." I felt like running out to the playground and calling out the same words.

However, Atticus had years to patiently raise his children. I have one year with the students in my class, and perhaps longer for those who go on studying with me on Saturday mornings. I needed to add to my class mission; to clarify precisely what I wanted my students to know even before they read *To Kill a Mockingbird,* now a year-ending class tradition. I didn't want to drop "There are no shortcuts," I simply wanted to refine my expectations. If my class produced brilliant students who were not equally good human beings, I had failed as a teacher. I was still stinging from the pain caused by the Musketeers, but I had enough distance to understand why I was hurt. It wasn't that they were upset or angry with me. It was that they had been mean and I had been mean right back. There was no kindness—not an ounce of gentleness behind their honesty, and gentleness is a desperately needed commodity in these days of hostility and boorishness. Yet how could I expect them to be sensitive when I had been insensitive, too? I knew kindness had to be part of my class mission, and that teaching the sort of kindness that lived in the heart of Atticus Finch would be the most difficult teaching challenge of all.

My mission statement was now complete. In addition to "There are no shortcuts," the class was now taught four additional words: "Be nice, work hard." I thought this phrase summed things up well. Not every student can be an algebra whiz, a virtuoso musician, or an all-star shortstop. Yet every student can be asked to try his best, and a good teacher or parent can work hard to model decency, humility, and compassion.

I was no longer anguished about the Musketeers; I was upset with myself for not having given them a chance to see a different type of human being. I did not want these children to be like everyone else, but I had never clearly shown them the possibility of a different kind of existence. I was upset because I had been a poor teacher.

Early in *To Kill a Mockingbird,* Jem refuses to come down from the tree house and eat breakfast because his father won't play football for the Methodists. Atticus goes out to invite Jem in to eat, but Jem refuses. Atticus doesn't get into a long discussion. He has made his offer and quietly walks away when Jem stubbornly declares he will not come down. "Suit yourself," says Atticus simply. He can rest easy because he's done his job as a loving father, and if Jem decides to go hungry, that's his choice. The wise father knows when to walk away and leave well enough alone.

As a teacher, I wish I had realized this early in my career, but at least I know it now. Whether I deal with administrators, parents, teachers, or students, I have my answer.

Years later, I was asked to give a series of talks to parents about reading. I brought along several students to demonstrate how we read literature in the classroom, and made suggestions to the parents watching as to how they could develop good readers in their homes. During the demonstrations, I often criticized today's public schools for making reading so incredibly boring (and that's not an easy thing to do).

Reports of my critical comments made their way back to the Jungle, and by eight o'clock the following morning I was summoned to the principal's office. The man was very angry and frustrated with me. I was chewed out for criticizing the schools. If this had happened years earlier, I would have been trying to fight my way out of the room.

But this was years later. I sat there and tried to see things from his point of view. He had done many good things as our principal. I knew he was furious with me, but he had also been good to me on more than one occasion. I was determined not to let his lecture block out times when I'd enjoyed his company.

I didn't tell this man that if he had read the Constitution lately he might have remembered that I had a right to my opinions. I might even have told him not to give me his opinion regarding the subject of reading, since I was probably a better reader than he. Instead, I remembered the mission of teaching my students to be nice and to work hard. Having a fight with this man wasn't going to get me any closer. So I nodded my head a lot, denied a few of his more serious accusations, and suppressed a laugh when he reminded me that the only reason I was a successful teacher was that "he made me." I thought to myself that my wife always told me the same thing. Then I shook his hand and thanked him for his concern. I told him I'd work hard and I appreciated having him for my boss.

Atticus has helped me out of other potential problems with fellow staff. He had to deal with Miss Debose, the next-door neighbor who terrorizes the Finch children by screaming all kinds of hateful threats as they walk down the street in front of her house. She screamed particularly disgusting remarks about their father. When Atticus sees her, he takes off his hat, compliments her into a stunned silence, and leaves with a simple "Well, it's grand seeing you, Miss Debose."

If Atticus had Miss Debose, I had Miss Mothball. A friend of mine once labeled her as part of a group of "83" teachers, meaning those who entered the lobby exactly when class began at 8:00 A.M. and left the minute school ended at 3:00 P.M.

She was a believer in self-esteem. That's fine, but her well-meaning attempts to never hurt a child's feelings were at best misled. In her efforts not to interfere with the inner child, her students simply ran around out of control for much of the day. Many subjects were not taught. The janitors hated to go into her room, which was so filthy it grew roaches large enough to walk off with school computers. Many of the schools I've visited have Miss Mothballs, who permit their students to run around, disrupting other classes. But merely telling your kids you love them isn't enough. As a friend once quipped to me, teachers like these have kids full of self-esteem, the "happiest group of illiterates on campus."

I was always polite to her. I didn't see any point in exhibiting my disgust with her teaching and my sadness for the children who suffered for a year in her filthy and disorganized classroom.

A few years ago a national magazine came to visit my classroom. A reporter had heard about the outstanding work the students were doing, and wanted to see for herself. She spent several days in class and then wrote an extraordinarily complimentary piece in a magazine not known for being particularly friendly to public education. She really hit the nail on the head, giving tremendous credit to the students themselves, who were so unusually nice and worked so incredibly hard.

The article generated thousands of letters to me from all sorts of people from around the world. Teachers, parents, and merely interested citizens had every kind of compliment for the children and interesting questions for me. It also enabled me to help other teachers do many of the things I was doing. I did, however, receive a hate letter.

Yes, it was from Miss Mothball. For three pages she detailed why I was a terrible teacher and an even worse human being. I'd received a few letters like this before and since, but this was the meanest of the lot. Although she had never been in my classroom, her letter questioned why so much attention was paid to my work when outstanding teachers like herself went unnoticed. I will leave out the personal viciousness this woman unleashed at me, although I had never said anything to her in my life except a friendly "Good morning" when I passed her in the hall. Her letter underscored the lesson my father had taught me when he tried to help me understand *Othello* at seven: never underestimate the power of jealousy.

I did, however, like the fact that after attacking my teaching, my integrity, and my abilities, she signed her letter "cordially."

The following day, I did indeed pass her in the hallway, and once again smiled and said, "Good morning." She refused even to look at me. That was fine with me. Atticus had shown me the way.

I must confess, however, that although I want so to be like Atticus, I all too frequently fall short of my goal. I made copies of her hate letter and sent them to many of my patrons who support a nonprofit foundation I had set up for my classroom. Upon reading it, some patrons increased their donations, writing back that if I had to teach with such a person, I needed all the support they could give me. Actually, I needed only Atticus, but the extra financial support came in handy!

The vast majority of parents I've encountered in eighteen years of teaching have been a pleasure to work with. Anyone who has raised children knows it can be the toughest job in the world, and I have been able to accomplish good things in school because I have the complete support of the parents. However, all teachers occasionally must encounter a parent they would prefer to forget. In the following case, Atticus did not merely guide me; he may have saved my life.

Mr. Jones and his family lived right across the street from the school. He had two delightful children. One was in my class, and the older daughter often spent her vacation breaks helping out by tutoring many of my students. These two young ladies were bright, beautiful, and talented. They had sunny dispositions and were extremely dependable. Joy, the little girl in my class, was always the first in my room each morning and the last one to depart for home at night.

There was a good reason for this, however. Her father terrorized both children and his wife. The authorities had been called many times, but there never seemed to be enough evidence to do anything with Mr. Jones. Joy often ran home at lunch to clean the house, as her father liked to hit her if he found any dust when he arrived home from his day at the local bar. He was often drunk, including the two times he came to school to have a parent conference with me. Joy would sit there and hang her head in shame. Joy's fragile mother never came to school. She worked seven days a week to support the family, cleaning homes and working in a nail salon.

Once I might have become involved in this situation and made things worse, but realistically, there was nothing I could say to this man to make him change his ways. Quietly, I told her father at the conferences that his daughter was a fine student and that he had every reason to be proud of her. He would grumble at me, blink his eyes hard, and stumble out of the room with Joy following. Still, she would be back the following morning at six o'clock, ready to work, with a shiny face and a courageous attitude.

Joy graduated from my class and went on to middle school. During her summer breaks she would spend a great deal of time back in my class, helping the younger children. One day she called the school hysterically from across the street. Her father had locked her in a closet and gone off with a shotgun after her mother, who was working at the nail shop. He had screamed that he was coming back for her after he dealt with the mother. Joy had escaped from the closet. I told her to call the police immediately and then come across the street. She was soaking wet when she arrived, as he father had held her underwater in their bathtub before locking her in the closet. My principal handled the crisis well and helped her hide. Some of the staff and I walked out to the school parking lot. We could see Joy's father in front of his apartment building with the gun in his hand. We didn't know if he had found his wife or not.

He didn't appear to be drunk; the way he walked indicated more fury than inebriation. Joy hadn't told me what had set him off that day, but it really didn't matter. I just remembered how frightened I was. I really thought he was going to kill me. Joy had told me how often he railed at her for wanting to spend so much time with me. He had resented me for years and now I was in range.

But he didn't shoot. He stared at me for a few moments from across the street as I waited motionless. I kept hoping the police would arrive and he would do nothing but scream at me in a foreign language. Sure enough, the police did arrive seconds later and got him to put down his weapon. I learned that day to appreciate police officers.

After two months of counseling he was allowed to return to his family, but conditions got worse and worse. Joy's mother finally escaped with her two daughters and was put in a safe house away from this man. Eventually the couple divorced.

Several years later, to my bewilderment, the father married another woman. Recently, while I was driving students home from a Dodgers game, I heard on the radio that there had been a multiple homicide across the street from the Jungle; some man had killed several people, his wife, and then himself. Names were not being disclosed pending notification of relatives, but I already guessed what had happened. The news was eventually released that Mr. Jones's new wife was trying to leave him and had brought her brother, her sister-in-law, and a friend to help her take her things. Joy's father had come home and killed them all before killing himself. I shuddered when I considered that this man really had been capable of pulling the trigger, and wondered why I had been so lucky. It's only a guess, of course, but I hope it's because I had always shown him respect when he abused me, because that's what Atticus would have done. Maybe he didn't kill me that day years ago because I had returned his anger and drunkenness with calm and respect.

Thank God Joy was no longer in the house. She's now graduated from college and leads a happy, productive life.

Most important of all, Atticus has helped me work with my students. Jane and Kim were an unusual pair of youngsters because they were both musical prodigies. Many teachers work for an entire career and never meet even one, and here I suddenly found myself with two. Both were brilliantly talented, and like so many others going through adolescence, both had their share of troubles. They had a good year in my class, though we were never exceptionally close. It was their choice; they didn't want to be close, and I no longer forced such an issue, even if I felt I could be of help. "Suit yourself," I would comment calmly when either of them wasn't participating in some activity I had arranged.

When they graduated from elementary school, I was able to arrange a scholarship for each of them at a private school with an outstanding music department. Fabulous young musicians came from all over the world just to go to this school. Its founder had become a special friend to me and arranged for these children from rather humble beginnings to have an opportunity normally reserved for children from privileged backgrounds.

Within a year I was hearing stories about Kim. She had lost interest in her studies and, more surprisingly, wasn't even enthusiastic about her music. The teachers at her school called me and asked me to speak with her before she threw away her scholarship.

I never made the call. I told the teachers that if Kim wanted to speak with me, she knew how to find me; she was at their school now and if they had any problem with her, it was their responsibility to handle it. As the years have gone by, I've heard stories of both hope and horror regarding Kim. She has had her ups and downs, like the rest of us. I still believe she will land on her feet. But it's not my job or business to get in touch with her and tell her what she should do. Kim knows how to find me if she ever needs help, and I will drop everything if she asks.

Of course I feel bad about this, but like Atticus, I can hold my head up. I was good to this young lady and, to this day, have fond feelings for her. I know so many young teachers and parents who blame themselves when things go wrong. I also know now that things can go wrong even when the parent or teacher does everything right. Such might have been the case with Kim.

Jane, on the other hand, began writing to me and calling me more often once she had left my classroom. Although she may have been the lesser of the two talents musically, she became an outstanding student at her new school and developed all kinds of eclectic interests and friends. Today she's in college and helps my class whenever she's in town. I never dreamed the class meant so much to her.

How foolish I was. I should have seen Jane's success coming much earlier. After all, for the last several years our most frequent communications have been through the mail. Her letters are always signed, "Love, Scout."

CHAPTER 8

A One-Story Town

So, after years of struggle and failure, you've reached the promised land. You have your mission and can't wait to fulfill it. You want kids who are special human beings, brilliant scholars, and young people who simply make the world a better place. Whether you have discovered Atticus or another beacon, you have your goal in sight. Better still, you know how to reach that goal.

And the kids can feel it. You're on a roll. The kids are excited and can't wait for you to lead them on a journey to excellence.

I have to give you some bad news. Even if you get to this point, the worst is yet to come. Even if lesser individuals than you have given up and you've stayed the course, even if you absolutely know you are ready to help young people change their lives for something truly special, the biggest hurdle is still in front of you.

I'm afraid that unless you are a very lucky teacher or parent, you and the children are most likely in the middle of a one-story town. It's bad enough if your town is also the home of mediocrity and ignorance, of apathy and occasionally even malice and evil. Yet a good teacher can find a way to overcome such an environment. But to paraphrase Henry Drummond in *Inherit the Wind,* ignorance and mediocrity are forever busy, and the forces of mediocrity aren't content with being mediocre; they'll do everything in their power to prevent even the humblest of teachers and children from accomplishing anything extraordinary. For good work shines a light on the failures of the mediocre, and that is a light which terrifies those who conspire to keep our nation's children, like themselves, ordinary.

Don't despair, though. You can't overcome the forces that work to prevent students from reaching the heights. But you will have to overcome them. And parents, this is the area where you can be of greatest service to your child's teacher and, of course, to your child himself.

It's my first day at a new school. I am beginning my third year of teaching, and the first at this incredibly crowded school in the middle of Los Angeles. There are forty sixth-graders in front of me. They come from Korea, Central America, Vietnam, the Philippines, and Thailand. None of them speaks English at home, and my best student reads at about a fourth-grade level. All of them have been in the United States for at least three years. They are absolutely as bright as the children of privilege I have left behind at the middle-class school where I spent my first two years of teaching.

After a few weeks, I have a plan to help them with English. I love Shakespeare. I am still a beginner in the classroom, but I have passion. I ask the kids if any of them would like to stay after school for an extra two hours a day to improve their English. I meet with their parents and tell them we're going to put on a Shakespeare play at the end of the year. I tell the parents that by learning English, their children can have better lives.

Five students and their parents bought in to the plan. These five children loved putting in the extra time and loved learning about Shakespeare. At first, their peers made fun of them every afternoon when they stayed behind at three o'clock as others went home. But these five were having so much fun learning that many of their peers wondered if maybe they were missing something. Within two weeks, I had twenty-eight of them working with me on *Macbeth*. They loved it, and we were having fun while learning.

However, my assistant principal at the time was concerned. The district hadn't given me permission to stay after school. And being a stupid third-year teacher, I made the biggest mistake a teacher can ever make: I asked permission.

As any experienced teacher will tell you, the first rule of teaching is *Never Ask Permission, Ask Forgiveness!* I, however, foolishly wrote a request to one of my supervisors downtown. I explained that for the rest of the year, twenty-eight students in my class would be working an extra ten hours a week after school. I didn't want to be paid. I would take care of all books and materials. We were simply doing extra work. These twenty-eight eleven-year-olds were going to perform *Macbeth* at the end of the year.

Within two days, my proposal came back. The rejection note was short. It said: "Mr. Esquith, it is not appropriate that you stay after school to teach Shakespeare. It would be better if you did something with the children that is *academic*."

I was speechless. And stupid. I actually listened to them. I was a coward and didn't want to upset the people downtown. At least I learned never again to ask permission.

I was still desperate to work on the English skills of my students and thought a play would be an effective way to do it after school. I tossed my Shakespeare idea aside for the time being and decided to do Thornton Wilder's masterpiece *Our Town*. I figured that with no sets and few costumes, it would be an easy play to produce. I also decided that I wasn't disobeying anyone, since Thornton Wilder wasn't William Shakespeare. Perhaps the district thought Thornton Wilder was academic. I sure wasn't going to ask permission and find out.

It was a terrific experience. The kids did a fabulous job. They really started to see just how far they could go with the educational bar raised higher. In fact, once we began working on the play, all of their subjects improved. Their concentration and focus were far better. Their attitude toward learning in general was outstanding.

The end of the year arrived, and that meant the night of our production. I proudly invited every supervisor I could find. Very few of them came, but one showed up from "downtown." The production was flawless—high school productions were no better than the work done by these sixth-graders.

The school official cried when Emily died. She cried when George broke down at her grave. And she cried when the stage manager pulled the curtain over the final scene. After a standing ovation, this official came up to me. She said, "Rafe, I've never seen Shakespeare done better."

That's a true story, and the schools are filled with people like this. Which is why, when you're in a one-story town, all your abilities and good intentions and hard work may still not be enough. Yet my class is proof that you can overcome this tyranny of the ordinary. But I've found it best to win such fights quietly, as Atticus would.

Usually, the battles in a school are small fights started by even smaller people. Such was the case with Miss Megabyte.

Miss Megabyte had been a teacher for over thirty years, and in many ways she was competent. In her class, everything had a place and there was a place for everything. Kids learned their skills and her room was a model of order. After years of teaching primary classrooms, she decided it was time for change and applied to become the teacher in the computer laboratory.

Many people believe that our schools are short of money, but that was certainly not the case with our large urban school. We always had lots of cash; we didn't always spend it wisely, but the money was there. We had an outstanding computer lab, and Miss Megabyte should be given high marks for organizing it and keeping it in good shape. It was her job to conduct several classes a day at the lab, teaching various lessons to different grade levels.

I liked her, but I always sensed she couldn't stand me. I was her worst nightmare. She had a grudging admiration for the students in my class, but I don't think she approved of my rebellious nature, particularly when I questioned district rules and regulations.

I have always demanded that my class have good manners, and people around the world have noticed that the children are particularly attentive and quiet when someone speaks to them. One week they walked into Miss Megabyte's computer lab and sat down in their assigned seats, waiting for her to give them the day's instructions.

"Well, what are you waiting for?" she asked them. "Turn on your computers and get to work!" They did so immediately.

The following week my students again entered her room quietly. I went with them. They sat down, turned on their computers, and began to work on the assignment she had given them the week before. "And who told you to turn on your computers?" she asked.

She was somewhat dictatorial, particularly the way she exerted control over the school's computers, including those not in the computer lab. She was a stickler for rules and regulations. One such episode stands out in my mind. It seems a teacher had committed an unpardonable sin. The school had provided each classroom with two new computers, and Mr. Spark had added a few extra fonts to the word-processing program the children used to write stories. For some reason Miss Megabyte entered his room and removed the fonts from his computers. Whew! I guess the world was still safe for democracy.

In fairness, I am sure she believed she was doing the right thing. The school district has rules about adding programs to computers that have not been approved as having educational value. Still, I believe most people (even those who work at the administrative level) would not have a problem with adding a couple of fonts to liven up the printed page.

Given this knowledge, I should not have been surprised at

what happened when I attempted to do a good deed for the school.

I have a friend named Mary who makes the human race look good. She's an important lawyer with a large company. When people like to attack greed and corruption, lawyers and businesspeople provide easy targets, and often the business community *should* be chastised for putting the dollar bill before human beings. However, it's been my experience that some lawyers and businesspeople are exactly the kind our country needs. Mary and her co-workers are such people. Each year, their firm spends hundreds of hours and thousands of dollars contributing funds to outstanding teachers and worthy programs all over town. Because of their efforts, there are disabled children who receive free swimming lessons and the transportation to get to them. Many school libraries have more books through their efforts. Mary's company brings children to the office to teach them about the business world, and she enjoys teaching the kids how to work phones, fax machines, and computer systems. The kids love Mary. She's a terrific role model who even invites children to her elegant home every year for a fun-filled Halloween party.

One day Mary's firm decided to put new computers in their office. They were going to get rid of sixty old ones that were too slow by current standards. Still, these were perfectly healthy computers on which any child could improve keyboarding skills and practice other tasks necessary to prepare for the future. Mary called me to ask if our school could use the computers. I thought it was a marvelous idea. I even went to a coordinator at the school, who was so excited she asked if she could keep one in her office. I called Mary and she set up the plan. She paid for a truck and had all the computers delivered on a Saturday so as not to disrupt a school day. The truck pulled into our parking lot. The coordinator had already decided with me which computer would go where. Teachers had been polled to find out who wanted an extra computer in his or her classroom. Students who were particularly needy were selected by teachers to come to school and pick up the first computer they would ever own. I kept no computer for my own class; I'm a lucky teacher and just wanted to share Mary's generosity.

Within a week the new computers had been removed from all the classrooms. Miss Megabyte confiscated all of them. Several teachers came to me very upset. It had been explained to them that it was against the rules to have computers in the classrooms which had not been approved by the district. These teachers weren't trying to threaten national security; they simply felt that with extra computers in their classes the kids would have more opportunities to improve their keyboarding skills.

It was a sad situation. Here we had a computer teacher depriving children of extra computers because, according to her understanding of the rules, every computer had to be the same with the same programs run in the same way. Some people were angry with Miss Megabyte, but I just felt sorry for her.

Atticus taught me that you have to stand in other people's shoes to understand where they are coming from. I strongly disagreed with Miss Megabyte, but I didn't protest or demand that the computers be replaced. I just decided that the fight wouldn't have been worth it, and that sooner or later all the children would have access to computers anyway.

She retired the following year. I occasionally think about

Miss Megabyte. Although she was very resentful of me, I had tried hard to be considerate and polite to her. It meant that when I told my students to "be nice," I could hold my head up and look them straight in the eye. Anyone can be nice to happy and pleasant people; I had done my best to be nice to Miss Megabyte. I had lost some computers, but knew I would be able to help my students continue to be nice. It was a small price to pay for something so valuable. I do not miss her, but I'm glad I knew her.

If you are a young teacher, consider the realities of working in a large school. Chances are, all sorts of people will ignore your most diligent efforts, and some, like Miss Megabyte, will upset you. You'll probably fail more than you succeed, and no one will come through your classroom door after twenty-five years with a basket of money to say thank you.

Be angry with this? Sure, go ahead and be angry. Just don't let the anger prevent you from being the teacher you want to be. As in athletics, most people do not perform at their best when angry. I met an outstanding young teacher years ago when I gave a staff development talk in an eastern state. He went on to use many of my teaching ideas and had a successful twelve years in the classroom. Yet one day he had had enough.

Another teacher in his school, jealous of his accomplishments, had actually written to parents of incoming students to try to persuade them not to let their children be assigned the following year to this excellent teacher. This young man, like me, used an extended day to help his students accomplish more. He was particularly successful with art, creating a superb after-school program in which he used his impressive creative talents to help children develop their own abilities. The fellow teacher called him a slave driver and warned the parents that a year with him could damage their children permanently.

When word got out about the letter, the accused teacher was furious. Most of his anger wasn't directed at the author of the letter but at his administrators, who hadn't fired the teacher who wrote it. There were several meetings with the two of them, both separate and together. Still, when the dust settled, the author of the letter had kept his job. The injured teacher was so angry that he filed a lawsuit against his co-worker, his school administrators, and his district. He became bitter and distant. His friends couldn't talk to him; they all wanted to know what he wanted. I'm not sure that he knew.

The point here is that since this mess happened, the teacher no longer teaches before and after school. He no longer comes in during vacations to do extra work. He is so angry at the system that he has decided to show them what they're missing. Of course, no one in the system cares, so his anger is Learlike, screaming to the deaf heavens.

And his kids have lost out. Having surrendered to his anger and the mediocrity of others, this fine young teacher will take his place among so many others who have quit going the extra mile. The best teachers are just as angry as my friend, but they put up with the lunatics for the sake of their students. That is not only reward enough, it's the only one a teacher will ever get, and the best teachers figure this out.

Many students around the world attend school on Saturday. In general, American children spend less time in school than their peers in other countries. It was years ago when students began studying with me Saturday mornings. They wanted to do some extra math and reading, and they enjoyed doing this work with friends in a happy environment rather than alone in what was often a home not conducive to scholastic pursuits. Eventually, this led to Saturday study for students who had graduated from the class and wanted to pursue excellence. They couldn't afford to take courses like the Princeton Review, and I was asked to help them level the playing field.

I didn't think this would be a problem. Many outside organizations used our school facilities on weekends. The local Korean community held Korean school Saturday mornings in many of our classrooms. Film companies shot television shows and even feature-length movies on our campus. Teachers often complained on Mondays because their classrooms had either been rearranged or were missing items ranging from pens and pencils to calculators and other expensive classroom supplies. Weekend visitors were asked by school officials to please keep an eye on things, but the problems continued.

When I went to my administrators to try to set up the Saturday morning program, they told me they had to think about it. Phone calls were made to supervisors downtown, and one woman was sent to inspect my idea and classroom. She had a fancy title that I forget, something like Director of Instructional Programs and Activities, but I felt it probably should have been Director of the California State Home for the Clueless. I knew I was in for a hard time when she asked to speak to my principal but expressed no interest in meeting any of the children who wanted to put in the extra time.

Finally, after about four months of consideration, the school decided to allow me to come in Saturday mornings and work with the students. They wanted to make sure I understood that I would not be paid (I never asked) and that, most important of all, I would not be allowed a key to open the gate of our school parking lot.

"Thank you for giving me the go-ahead for the Saturday program," I told them gratefully. "But may I ask you why I can't have a key for the parking lot?"

Here came the line all good teachers know all too well: "Rafe, if we gave *you* a key, we'd have to give *everyone* a key, wouldn't we?"

No, I thought to myself, you wouldn't have to give everyone a key. You could tell other teachers that they, too, could have a key if they were willing to come in and teach for free on Saturdays. I was angry. But I left Roy Hobbs behind years ago. I was upset, but I knew why I was standing outside the school gates keyless on a Saturday morning. Fifty students patiently waited outside on an unusually cold, drizzly California day.

I can take the crap. Atticus took a lot more of a pounding than I have ever had to withstand. People spat at him. They threatened and cursed his children. Bob Ewell even tried to kill Jem and Scout. But Mr. Finch had a cause and stayed focused so he could do his best for his children. May that be said for all parents and teachers.

Ten minutes late, a janitor arrives (he has been with our school less than a year and has been given a key). He returns my cheerful "Good morning" with an unenthusiastic grunt, and my students file into school and up to class.

I don't have a key, but fifty students work all morning, surviving the horrors of *Titus Andronicus* and putting up with my bad jokes and attempts to make the SAT seem fun. I have to hurry because that night Barbara and I are throwing our annual holiday dinner and casino party for sixty children at our house.

The students pack up their supplies at noon, but I'm stopped as we're almost out the door. Jenny, a former student from last year's Saturday program, has come to see me with some news. She's received her PSAT results, and she's been chosen as a National Merit Scholar.

Her eyes and smile pierce me. It's a one-story town, but Atticus and not Roy lives there. Joy has replaced anger.

CHAPTER 9

A Touch of Gray

I do not envy parents who try to support public education. You want the best for your child. Realistically, you are aware that a Socrates cannot teach every class, and you understand that not every teacher is going to send your child home every day thrilled about going to school. However, far too often inexperienced teachers who aren't up to the challenge are leading our classrooms. Even when young teachers are outstanding, they're often so discouraged after a couple of years that they leave teaching, creating a cycle of inexperience. Parents need to be supportive of their child's teacher. Even the best young teachers feel alone, and support and appreciation from parents can mean the difference between a young instructor blossoming and remaining on the job for many years or one of the countless teachers who quit within their first three years. I am selfish. If we can develop fine teachers, they will send me students who are ready to continue the quest to end cycles of poverty and ignorance. If we continue to chase away some of our best young instructors, schools and children will continue to fail.

It's fun to play the blame game while wringing our hands about education: parents aren't raising their children properly; television has ruined the kids; the teachers are terrible; society doesn't want to fund education properly. It's an easy game to play.

And there's some truth to all these accusations. But a key reason our teachers aren't getting the job done is that good people often no longer stay in teaching. If you enter a large campus in any urban area, you'll be surprised at the ages of the teachers. They are very young, novices in a profession where experience can mean the difference between success and failure.

The schools are hiring practically anyone who breathes, and a friend of mine who is a principal says that the standard is even lower than that! All kinds of young people are being hired. Some of them have real talent, some of them care, yet few of them will remain teachers for more than a couple of years.

Others are being hired who became teachers only because they didn't know what to do with their lives. They figure they'll teach for a year or two and then move on to their *real* jobs. They spend their days looking at the school calendar, calculating the number of days until vacation when they can ski or go to Europe.

And through it all, the kids suffer.

We have dozens of new young teachers this year at the Jungle, and I get to see a handful of them on a regular basis. Many have the goods to become top-notch. Each year these young people are like so many other new teachers walking into classrooms all over the country—classes filled with students whose previous teachers have rarely had a touch of gray. And no matter what year and what place, young teachers share experiences that are sadly similar.

It is Miss Hummingbird's first day with her fourth-graders. Her class is quite wild, and Miss Hummingbird knows she needs to lay down the law right away to establish control. She is attractive and has a warm personality, and within a few hours the class has found its rhythm and all is going well. One boy, however, is doing no work and paying no attention. Several times during the day, Miss Hummingbird talks to him and tries a variety of strategies to get him on task. Finally, she decides to let him know that his actions will have consequences.

She walks over to the young man, who is throwing spitballs while everyone else in the class is completing a math assignment. Miss Hummingbird quietly and calmly says to him, "Albert, this is a desk. Do you know why we have a desk in school? We use it to do work. As you are not doing any work, you may stand up and other students in our class will use it. Thank you very much."

Albert stands up and takes a step back from his desk. Miss Hummingbird pushes his chair in and says, "Thank you, Albert. When you're ready to do work, I will let you sit down and begin. But make no mistake about it, I make the rules here, and you will work when I tell you to work. I like you and know you can do a good job. Do you understand me?"

"Yes," says Albert.

"Well, you just stand there for a few minutes while I help your classmates do their work. Maybe then you'll be ready to work as well." Miss Hummingbird then turns to another student. Within fifteen seconds several students are screaming.

Miss Hummingbird turns around and sees something for which she is definitely not prepared. Albert has dropped his pants and underwear and is flashing her. Now it is Miss Hummingbird who screams. She runs from the classroom to get me, and I help her calm things down. She's in complete shock that a fourth-grader would do such a thing. Soon we have Albert (with his pants on) in an assistant principal's office, and Miss Hummingbird is back in her class, shaken but ready to resume.

Later, when we discuss what happened, I console her by telling her that she did nothing wrong. I tell her that she's experienced something very rare and it was just particularly unfortunate that it happened to her on her first day of teaching. I also stress that she should try to learn from everything that happens, both good and bad. I then ask her what she might do if it were to happen again.

"I think I might laugh and get out my tape measure," she quips. Miss Hummingbird has a sense of humor when all is going wrong. She's ready to become a first-rate teacher.

One year brought us Miss Busy-as-a-Bee, equally enthusiastic and capable. Her first class is a predominantly rough group of fifth-graders. Most of them are rude and not very bright. Despite her intense efforts, the class is making little progress.

Miss Busy-as-a-Bee is at school each morning by 6:15. Her lesson plans are thorough and carefully constructed. If she were in a middle-class school she'd be an instant success, but it would be difficult even for a seasoned veteran to make much progress with this class. The children are reading at a first-grade level and few of the students know their multiplication tables. Miss Busy-as-a-Bee's chances with this group are slim.

Still, she's a tough young kid, and practically nothing gets her down. She begins staying an hour after school several days a week and keeping her class open so students who wish to may get help with homework. As she lacks a graduate teaching credential, she leaves immediately after her homework club to attend boring classes run by the school district to train new teachers who haven't attended graduate school.

Since Miss Busy-as-a-Bee is new, she is assigned a mentor teacher. New teachers are assigned these supervisors to help them learn the ropes. Unfortunately, Miss Busy-as-a-Bee has been assigned a man the novice teachers jokingly call "the Inspector."

Let's give Inspector Irving some credit: he never misses a day of school and he takes his job seriously. Many schools have bureaucrats like this, who often make the mistake of confusing seriousness with effectiveness. Oftentimes, however, such people are not the best teachers and are not the best people to use as mentors.

Inspector Irving, for example, can often be seen screaming at his own students to gain control of his class. This makes it difficult for teachers like Miss Busy-as-a-Bee to take him seriously when, with all the best intentions, he advises her on matters of classroom management. On more than one occasion, Miss Busy-as-a-Bee has felt hurt by being criticized by someone whose class is in no better shape than her own. These hurt feelings have her considering leaving the profession, something that frequently happens when good young teachers become discouraged by what they believe to be absurd interference with their attempts to teach.

Inspector Irving observes a reading lesson Miss Busy-as-a-Bee is teaching. Our young teacher follows the text exactly as she has been asked to do, given that Inspector Irving is glowering at her from the back of the room. The lesson goes well. All of the students remain on task, understand the material, and do their best for Miss Busy-as-a-Bee. The bell rings and the students are dismissed to recess, as the nervous young instructor remains in the room to be evaluated by the Inspector. At this moment Miss Busy-as-a-Bee would prefer being in a marine barracks with the DI checking for dust under her cot.

The Inspector, however, says nothing about the lesson at all. There is no discussion of the children, their understanding of the material, nor the manner in which this fine young instructor has related to the children. These are issues of no interest to this mentor teacher. Instead, the Inspector focuses on the lesson plan that is supposed to be placed on Miss Busy-as-a-Bee's desk. These plans, including a schedule and list of objectives for a class, are clearly printed inside the teacher's guides. A teacher can easily xerox a plan and place it on her desk. Most teachers do have a copy on their desks, and the new teacher has one. But Inspector Irving is not happy: he wants Miss Busy-as-a-Bee to copy the lesson plan out of the book in her own handwriting. This will take about thirty minutes a day. When Miss Busy-as-a-Bee protests that this is a pointless waste of valuable time, Inspector Irving frowns and threatens her with a poor evaluation if she refuses to copy the plan. Consequently, the new teacher spends every lunch hour practicing her own handwriting.

Still, Miss Busy-as-a-Bee survives her first year and has

done a fine job. It's the last Friday and the school is having a minimum day, meaning classes will be dismissed at 12:20 P.M. instead of the traditional 3:00. New classes will be entering their rooms in a mere fifty-six hours. There is no summer break at a year-round school.

During recess on their first year's final Friday, the rookie teacher receives a notice from the district. The district doesn't have all the proper paperwork from her and if it doesn't receive the items by 3:00 P.M. that day, she will not have a job Monday morning. She panics and races downtown when school ends. She finds herself standing in line with hundreds of other new teachers who have received the same threat. All of these young teachers are treated with shocking rudeness by many of the district personnel. It would be nice if the district had someone behind the desk saying something to the tune of "I'm so sorry you're going through this hassle. We're grateful for your long hours and hard work to help the children have better lives. We know this paperwork is ridiculous and we're going to help you all we can so you will be able to get out of here and have a relaxing weekend." Perhaps Richard Kiley could then stop in and sing "The Impossible Dream."

Instead, by the time she gets to the front of the line, people tell her she's too late—it's almost five o'clock and everyone is going home. She might still be able to teach on Monday if she comes back early Saturday morning, when some office people will help a few of the teachers keep their certification.

Our heroine returns Saturday morning at 4:30 to find more than fifty new teachers waiting in line or sleeping on benches. She manages to get to the front of the line in time, but after filling out the proper forms, she's informed that the district needs her fingerprints. When Miss Busy-as-a-Bee explains that she was fingerprinted at the beginning of the year, the district official tersely informs her that they have no such record and she will have to do it again, which involves another office and more lines. She goes through the hassles, survives the day, but is hard-pressed to turn up Monday morning in a cheerful mood to meet the new students. Time will tell if one day, when her hair is gray, she'll still be at the door to meet a new group of children.

Mr. Baseball doesn't start off as quickly as Miss Hummingbird or Miss Busy-as-a-Bee. He has more ideas than either of them but quickly learns that his students are lacking in so many areas that his planned activities are going to have to be shelved for quite some time while reality sets in. The children like him—he's warm, amusing, and they find him interesting. He's often seen after school shooting hoops with his class or tossing around a football. Many of his students don't have a father, and they like being around a good guy who cares about their futures. Mr. Baseball has hoped to encourage young people to write, as he himself is an enthusiastic writer and has given a lot of thought to developing the writing process in the minds of his children. He isn't prepared for a class of ten-year-old children who cannot write a complete sentence in any language. The third week of school brings to class DARE, or Drug Abuse Resistance Education, a well-intentioned program sponsored by police officers across the country to teach children the dangers of drug abuse. Officers visit the classrooms for a series of weekly lessons teaching children to say no to drugs. Like so many programs, DARE is only as good as the person leading the lessons. Mr. Baseball's class is fortunate in having an interesting and caring officer who does a good job.

Each week the session opens when the DARE officer answers anonymous questions that have been placed in the DARE box. This way, kids can get accurate answers to questions that are troubling enough to prevent their being asked openly in front of peers. Kids often ask questions about the law because they're afraid of what might be happening to an older sibling or a parent. However, during the first DARE lesson, the first question opened by the officer asks, "Do you like pussy?" The second asks what oral sex tastes like. Mr. Baseball's class may not write complete sentences, but they do write interesting questions. Mr. Baseball spends his lunch hour contemplating the state of the ten-year-old mind-set in urban Los Angeles today. The children's knowledge of sex and other things that were once considered strictly adult is frightening to all who work in schools today.

Mr. Baseball is scared, and he should be. He has been instructed, as all teachers are now instructed, never to touch a child. Don't pat them on the head. Don't give them a hug. For God's sake, *never* be alone with a child. He knew teaching would be difficult, but he wasn't prepared for the fact that everyone in school is frightened because of the attention now focused on the touching of children. He has heard all the stories of teachers and others who have been accused of improperly touching a youngster. He knows that if any of his students were ever to accuse him of something, his life would be over. The legal authorities would have to take the accusation seriously because the child must be protected. The school administrators have to cooperate with a police investigation or be accused of covering up what might be a serious crime. Whether or not an accusation would be true,

Mr. Baseball has been correctly warned that he loses the moment the accusation is made.

Of all the students in the class, it is Bobby who most adores Mr. Baseball. Bobby doesn't have a father, his mother works nights; he comes home to an empty house. Consequently, he stays at school long after the dismissal bell has rung. He plays basketball even after the sun has gone down, when the only people left on the playground are the omnipresent gangsters who, vulturelike, hang out to prey on the elementary kids. Bobby asks Mr. Baseball if he can play with him after school. His teacher wants to stay, but the rest of the class has left for home before darkness falls. Mr. Baseball leaves too, because the risk is too great. This evening, like most others, Bobby will be on the playground alone.

One year Mr. Incompetent is hired because he speaks a particular language and thus is hopefully able to teach a specific national group at our school. His English, however, is so poor that few can understand him when he tries to communicate. He has a very good mentor teacher who encourages him to decorate his room. He puts up a chart he has created to help students with their writing. Its title is WHAT MAKE A GOOD SENTENCE. Rule 1 states "It Starts With a capital Letter." Is it any wonder his students are having difficulty with their writing skills?

I'm sorry to be tough. Being a first-year teacher is hard enough, but we're hiring lots of Mr. Incompetents these days. They range from lazy people to hard workers, but the truth is many of these people do not have the goods ever to be quality teachers. They don't connect with their students, they don't have the necessary education to be good instructors, and they are not held accountable for their failure. Teaching is one of those rare jobs in which too many circumstances, people who perform poorly are allowed to continue.

Yet the hiring of people who do not have the necessary skills is not the worst of it. We do hire young people with good, and sometimes outstanding, potential. Miss Bright Light is a remarkable young woman and born to be a teacher. She's highly intelligent and educated. She's extremely well read and cares deeply about her students. She sets the bar high. She is also determined to improve herself, so she constantly spends time with some of the better veteran teachers, observing their classrooms and picking their brains. She is good—really good—but knows she can be so much better.

Some in the school administration do not like her. She asks too many questions. She often engages people in philosophical discussions. She doesn't salute every time one of the administrators walks by.

One year Miss Bright Light gets wonderful news. She has been accepted into the doctoral program of education at one of the world's premier universities. She will attend the program for a year and get her Ph.D. She then plans to return to our school. What a feather in an elementary school's cap! A highly respected doctor of education would be on the staff of a large urban school.

But an administrator tells her that if she leaves to attend the graduate program, she can forget about coming back: he needs her *now*. He's been working hard to make the school run efficiently and he's losing a good teacher, so he tells Miss Bright Light that she's lucky to have been given a job, and that people who leave aren't welcome to return after displaying such ingratitude. You'd think this administrator would kiss her feet—you'd think he would thank the education gods for providing someone young and brilliant to help our children. Instead, he tells her not to let the door hit her ass on her way out.

And she is gone. How many of our young students could have benefited from this fine young teacher? No matter. Mr. Incompetent will teach her class next year.

CHAPTER 10

When Numbers Get Serious

I used to teach with one of the kindest men I have ever known, but he gave his students A's in arithmetic every year when in fact his class could barely add. I once asked him about this practice, and he said that if his students felt good about themselves, they'd become good math students one day. Since teachers are rarely held accountable for their actions, this practice went on for years. His students were actually convinced they were good mathematicians. Later in life they no doubt found out the truth the hard way.

We must be honest with our students. The truth will motivate students to work harder at their math. You don't have to be an ogre to be straight with your students. Good teachers tell their students when work is not good enough, but couple this verdict with optimism and encouragement and the message that better results are within reach.

Many adults remember being tortured by mathematics. We remember struggling late at night over algebra that was a complete mystery. For many of us, geometry's axioms and corollaries may as well have been the Dead Sea Scrolls.

In my early years in the classroom, I noticed two things about children and numbers. The first was that most young children love arithmetic and can do it quite well. Numbers are a universal language. Even at the Jungle, where language barriers often hindered students from becoming good readers and writers, math scores were usually quite good. Sadly, the second fact that caught my attention was that many children who did well in arithmetic at the elementary level declined in middle school. I knew the children were bright, so their intelligence wasn't the issue.

One day I was chosen to coach a math team for the Jungle in a citywide competition. I had had the experience of being in charge of such a project at my previous school. In a memo I asked teachers to send me students who they felt would represent our school well; I was to pick six of them to be on the squad.

A well-respected teacher came to me immediately. Miss Egghead told me that my search was over: she had the six finest math students in the school, and she was certain they would lead us to glory. As a new teacher, I was grateful for her help and brought the six to my room, where I gave them ten sample problems to do. They were to solve them cooperatively and turn in a single set of answers. They missed them all.

I went back to Miss Egghead and thanked her for her support but informed her that other children would be representing the school. She furiously snatched the test results out of my hand and glared at the test paper. With a look of

Eureka! in her eyes she exclaimed, "Well, no wonder they missed them! You gave them *word problems*. I haven't taught the children to solve such word problems this year— we've only done math."

That began my education about what sometimes passes for the teaching of numbers in public schools today. Of course, many teachers work hard to teach the children the importance of numbers, but many others, more than any school would like to admit, either teach arithmetic poorly or sometimes don't teach it at all.

My fifth-grade students have been in school long enough to tell tales of both good and bad experiences. In some of their classes the teachers simply skipped arithmetic altogether on many days. Teachers often assigned them basic computation but left undone sections of the textbooks that required problem-solving skills and higher-level thinking. These problems may be skipped because they demand more work for the teacher or, worse, because the teacher himself doesn't understand how to solve them.

Teachers like these sometimes had difficulty with numbers when they were in school, and have continued the cycle in their own classrooms.

I recently attended a staff development session in teaching arithmetic, at which the facilitator warmed up the audience with some simple mental math exercises. The majority of the elementary teachers solved them, but the responses of a fair number of people sitting near me were frightening when one considers that children's arithmetic skills are under their tutelage. The session leader called out the following questions and actually received the answers in parentheses: "17 minus 11" ("7") and "the square root of

100" ("50"). A good many teachers in the room gave answers like these. Our group leader corrected them; several laughed out loud and joked, "Well, it's not like we have to be gifted or something."

No, these teachers are not the rule, but they are not a shocking exception, either. There are many teachers in our system who can't do basic arithmetic and show no desire to better themselves for the sake of their students. I wonder if our society would be tolerant of general medical practitioners who didn't know their basic anatomy. Yet we tolerate ignorant teachers and are paying a terrible price for our apathy.

This is not intended to be a how-to book for young teachers, but one idea has been so successful in my class that I would like to share it with parents and teachers. It's an all-encompassing class economic system that not only helps students understand important concepts in arithmetic but also deals with classroom behavior and teaches the children valuable skills to help build their characters and their futures. Versions of the program are now being used in many classrooms around the country and by parents at home.

As with most successful teaching ideas, this one developed in stages rather than all at once. It was born out of my own personal financial difficulties and a former student who, brilliant though he was, couldn't do his laundry.

In one of my first classes, Young was one of the cleverest and most delightful students it had ever been my pleasure to teach. He was studious, curious, and had a generosity of spirit that made him a recognized leader. His mother worked in a sweatshop seven days a week and raised him by herself. But he managed to overcome all obstacles and was accepted into one of the nation's finest colleges. He had always been a computer whiz and even built his own computer out of spare parts when he was eleven years old.

During his first week away at college, he called me and told me he had a serious problem. Before he could even say what it was, I was planning to send him the money he must be needing or give him the emotional support he was seeking for some crisis he was having his first time away from home. Instead, this highly intelligent boy couldn't figure out why his underwear had turned pink in the wash! It turned out that Young, who could do calculus in his head and thought physics was boring because it was too easy, didn't know how to separate his lights from his darks.

Later that night, as I chuckled myself to sleep, I was thankful that he hadn't asked me for money, because I was broke as usual. And it occurred to me how much time I spent thinking about my bleak financial situation, and how upset I was with myself for foolishly spending money I didn't have.

Young always told me I was his favorite teacher, but I began to ask myself why this was so. True, he had a wonderful year in my class. I had taught him some important academic lessons, and perhaps I had supplied a little extra kindness to his already gentle soul, but I began to think about how a good teacher must be measured. It was an epiphany, and I never slept that night. I came to see that a good teacher gives a student skills that are used not only in class but through the rest of his life.

I sat up all night wondering what skills I could give students to help them in the years to come. It was easiest to examine my own failures and pass on any lessons I had learned to help my students avoid the same traps. And my class economic system was born.

On the first day of school, each child has to apply for a job. Application forms are passed out, and the students must fill them out. For the more demanding jobs, such as banking, a student has a couple of days to get a letter of reference from another teacher or adult to confirm that he or she would be dependable.

Here is the list of jobs (and the pay that goes with each) from which the children choose their occupations:

Banker, $600

A banker keeps records for four to six students in the class. This student must be good at arithmetic and a person of the highest integrity. The banker takes deposits and checks from the bank customers and coordinates accounts with the other bankers. There are usually five or six bankers in my class.

Janitor, $650

A janitor is given a specific area of my room to keep spotless. One scrubs the sink daily. Two children sweep the room at least twice a day. Others wax cabinets or scrub desks. They are highly paid because I want a dazzling classroom, one that sparkles at all times. Thanks to the janitors, I spend no time organizing or cleaning my own room. I spend each moment of my day teaching.

Grader, $575

I have student graders for two subjects: grammar and spelling. The work I give in these two areas is objective and can be graded by any fair person with an answer sheet. Again, for the sake of time management, having student graders frees my assistant and me to spend our time teaching or grading writing assignments that only we are qualified to handle. Spelling graders take home Friday's spelling tests and return them to me graded on Monday morning. Grammar graders collect homework in the

Messenger, $525

Police Officer, $500

Video Monitor, $575

morning and return graded assignments after recess.

We usually have two students who handle all errands to other classes or the office. These students must be able to deliver oral messages accurately and must know the school staff.

A police officer has several duties. Each one patrols a selected area of the room. The officer has a book with the names of all the students in his jurisdiction. If a student breaks any of the class rules, the officer keeps a record of the infraction. The officer helps me collect all the fines that students pay for breaking rules. I usually have three to five police officers.

The video monitors keep our collection of more than four hundred videos and DVDs organized in our library. They are responsible for checking these out to students on Fridays and for collecting video work and videos Monday mornings.

Recycler, $550 We usually have two monitors to recycle our waste. Cans are taken each day to the recycling bin.

Attendance Monitor, $475 This student must have outstanding attendance. The monitor silently takes attendance each morning and accepts notes from returning students to be kept on file. This is a very boring job in my class, as 99 percent of the students will never miss a day of school the entire year! (It's not that they don't get the flu—they insist on coming with it.)

Clerk, $550 I usually have about three students who are my official clerks. These students pass out and collect papers. They

Ball Monitor, $485

Librarian, $525

also keep my materials organized and know where everything in my closet is stored. This student takes care of all our athletic equipment. This includes not only our baseballs and volleyballs but weights used for aerobic training. This student is in charge of the class library of Newbery Medal winners that we use for book reports. Students go to the librarian to return or check out books.

The children are told that in my class everyone works. Why? Because they have to pay rent to sit at their tables! The class is set up with five or six islands of tables. I seat the kids facing one another as much as possible—it fosters friendships and cooperation. After an early class discussion, the islands are given names, usually based on a theme the children have suggested. The areas of the room closer to the front have higher rents than the ones in the back. For example, one year my class named our islands after parts of Los Angeles:

Bel-Air

Front of the room—$1,000 a month to sit here

Beverly Hills	Middle of the room—$750 to sit here
Hollywood	Next to our video library—$700 to sit here
Santa Monica	Near the water fountain—$675 to sit here
Skid Row	Back of the room—$550 to sit here

Another year we used the names of department stores for our areas: Bloomingdale's, Saks Fifth Avenue, Macy's, Sears, and Kmart (it helps to have a sense of humor).

Payday and Rent

Payday is the last Friday of each month. Each student receives a set of checks at the beginning of the year. I used a computer to create Jungle checks. I teach the students how to fill out a check and how to deposit one in a bank. I also give each child a sheet for keeping banking records.

As you've probably noticed, in our economic system rent exceeds even the highest pay. If the students can't pay their rent at the end of the month, they're evicted from their seats and have to sit on the floor. How can a child save enough money to afford the monthly rent? The answer lies in a system of incentive payments we call bonus money. Students can earn bonus money by doing well in class, displaying outstanding citizenship, and participating in certain optional activities. Conversely, our police officers will fine students if rules are broken. Following are lists of bonus opportunities and fines levied on any student who doesn't toe the line:

Bonus Money

$50	Perfect spelling test (after three in a row, the amount doubles)
$50	90 percent on any other test
$200	100 percent on any other test
$50	Completing a weekend video assignment
$100	Perfect attendance for the month
$100	Coming to school early for extra math
$100	Staying after school for Shakespeare
$100	Joining the school orchestra
$100	Joining the school chorus
$100	Playing guitar with Rafe during recess and lunch
$200	Being complimented by another teacher

Fines (these double when offenses are repeated)

$50	Tardy (this doubles with each offense)
$50	Missing homework
$50	Rudeness, such as not listening when another student is speaking
$100	Messy desk (discovered in police raids)
$500	Dishonesty

Bonus money and fines are distributed and collected as "cash." I make money on a computer and print it on card stock at the local Kinko's. I change colors every year so students can't borrow from the previous class. This part of the program also teaches the students to take care of their cash and understand the security of a checking account.

Purchase of Condominiums

Now the fun really begins. At any time a student may purchase his seat and call it a condominium. Paying the bank three times the amount of his rent can do this. For example, if the rent is $800 per month, a $2,400 check to the bank makes the student the official owner of his seat. From that time on, the student no longer has to pay rent each month. This teaches the students how to save their money and the advantages of owning instead of renting property.

But that's not all. Students may buy another person's rented seat and become a landlord. If a student buys another person's seat, then the student renting the seat must pay his landlord every month. As you can imagine, students are highly motivated to earn and save their money. They find out quickly that the rich really do get richer when they work hard and plan ahead. Incidentally, we have rent control in our class, because some landlords tend to raise the rents through the roof!

It gets deeper still. Students who own seats must pay property taxes every December 10 and April 10. This is figured into the income-tax returns all students fill out by April 15. They learn mathematics, bookkeeping, economic responsibility, and tax structure. And they have lots of fun doing it.

Auctions

At the end of the month, after paychecks have been deposited and rents paid, we have a wild auction. School supplies, art materials, books, and athletic equipment are just some of the things sold. The kids learn all kinds of lessons here. They scream, shout, and compete with a fury that might intimidate an experienced Wall Street trader. Some children spend all their money on buying things, others wisely hold off because they're saving for their condominiums. Still others never buy anything until the end of the year, because they know I reserve some of the coolest items until the last month. In this way, students learn about saving, planning, and the most important concept of all, delayed gratification.

Many parents I know use parts of this system at home with their children. I often hear about kids who don't keep their rooms clean or complete other household chores. With this system, nagging is no longer necessary. Children at home can get an allowance; however, as in real life, allowances are paid only if work gets done. If a child is expecting $5 on Saturday, but it was made clear that the $5 will be paid for helping with the dinner dishes, keeping the bedroom clean, or coping with laundry, there is no need to nag the child to finish the work: if the work isn't completely done, no allowance is due. There's nothing to discuss and no lecture to give. A simple and friendly "suit yourself" à la Atticus Finch gets the point home.

If your child then needs money for a movie or some other activity with friends, the answer is no. He had his chance to earn his allowance and failed to do so. Our children today not only have forgotten how to *pursue* life, liberty, and happiness, but unfortunately have replaced the word "pursue" with "entitled." It's our duty as teachers and parents to let our children understand that movies and dances are terrific, but they aren't rights guaranteed by the Constitution. They are privileges and should be earned. It's not a discussion. It's the way things are, and the sooner our children understand this, the more successful they will be in life.

A good thing about our classroom economics is that it allows children to be creative. Phillip was an incredibly enterprising young man. He actually created an insurance company and wrote policies for children to cover their fines. If a child often missed homework assignments, Phillip would create a policy to cover the fines up to a certain amount of money per month. This became particularly hilarious when one student came to Phillip to write a policy to cover fines for tardiness. Phillip checked the kid's attendance records and turned him down, saying firmly, "I'm sorry, but you're a bad risk." Phillip made a fortune with his insurance company. Today he majors in business at an outstanding university.

A creative and provocative student named Ken exploited the class economic system in an even more amusing way. Kenny was very bright but one of the laziest kids I had ever known, constantly forgetting to finish his homework, and his fines mounted. By the third month of class he was going to lose his seat. I had a conference with Kenny's mom to get her approval to put him on the floor. She was all in favor of it—she had the same problems with her son at home; she adored him, but he drove her crazy. All through our conference, Kenny readily admitted that he was lazy and was more than willing to accept his punishment.

The following morning I arrived at school at my usual 6:15, but Kenny was already there, standing by the classroom door with a homemade sign around his neck: "*I am a Vietnam vet and need help.*" He put the bite on every kid who entered the room that day with his cup in his hand and his eyes pleading for charity. By the end of the day he had raised enough money to pay his fines and get his seat back. I wasn't sure I approved of his strategy, but I had to give him credit for ingenuity.

Today Kenny makes independent films. He is an excellent fund-raiser.

When all is said and done, a good teacher helps the student to improve the quality of his life. With so many children growing up poor, one of my major goals is to give that child a fighting chance to end the cycle of poverty that paralyzes hopes and dreams. It's not enough to ask kids to pull themselves up by their bootstraps—many of them don't even know what bootstraps are. With our schoolroom economic system, students learn to value and take care of property and to plan ahead and earn the things they want. With luck they'll go on to use these economic skills for the rest of their lives. I still hope that one day some of my students will look back and reflect that their year with me was one of their best. But more important, I hope their reflecting is done in their own homes. As Malcolm X wrote, I know my students are *in* America. I want them to be *of* America, too.

CHAPTER 11

One

E ddie is a brilliant student. He is a small child from El
Salvador who has been been in the United States for
fewer than three years and speaks English fluently. He
is funny, kind, exuberant, and has an incredible aptitude for
mathematics. He is the obvious choice to be captain of the
math team that will compete against other schools. In fact,
he constitutes an entire squad by himself. It is no surprise,
therefore, that at the competition on a Saturday in spring he
wins first place in every event and dominates all comers.

The following Monday our school has an assembly, and
Eddie is brought in front of over a thousand students to
have his extraordinary accomplishments saluted. All of the
administration and teachers are so proud and happy for him.

An hour later I sit in the nurse's office comforting him.
Five or six of his peers who do not share the staff's enthusi-

asm for his victory gave Eddie a bloody nose and a split lip. Welcome to the world of the gifted child.

What should we do with children of high and sometimes extraordinary abilities in a system that nurtures mediocrity? I've been fortunate to work with gifted and talented (GATE) students for eighteen years now. By sticking around so long and meeting kids like Eddie, I've learned a few things. I could see that there were students at the Jungle with outstanding abilities, but not only did the school sometimes fail to help them develop their abilities; talented students sometimes were quite actively discouraged from showing what they could accomplish. And not just by their peers. People at every level of the school blocked progress for the brightest youngsters.

In my first year, I had eight GATE students out of the forty in my class. The selection process, based on IQ or several years of outstanding achievement in the classroom and on standardized tests, was run by a committee of administrators, teachers, and parents. Clustering places GATE students in a regular classroom but does not provide special instruction—the teacher provides the special instruction (or not). Other schools pull such children out of their normal classes for part of the day, in the same way students leave to go practice with an orchestra or chorus. Other schools simply put all GATE students together in one class.

Good teachers at our school helped find talented kids. Many of the staff would come to the selection committee and say, "I've got a kid whose interests would be best served in a program of differentiated and specialized instruction." In this way, caring teachers acted as a kind of scouting system for teachers like me who were trying to create opportunities for gifted youngsters. These scout teachers gave time after school to sit on the selection committee and ensure that kids they had discovered would have the opportunity to go on to accomplish great things. They felt proud of unearthing "rough jewels" who, if polished, could go on to brighten the world.

But for every scout, there was a teacher who did everything possible to undermine the efforts of advocates for gifted children. When a child was supposed to transfer from a class with a traditional curriculum into a class with other gifted children, the selection committee would often have the following conversation with a teacher:

Committee: Hi. We've got some great news. Billy has qualified for a GATE class. You should be really proud of him.

Miss Plug: But you can't take Billy. He's my best helper.

Committee: What do you mean?

Miss Plug: I can't get by without him. He grades all my papers and cleans my room.

Committee: Well, with all due respect, that's not why he's here in school.

Miss Plug: But he's the one who sparks my classroom.

Committee: Actually, isn't that your job?

Miss Plug [angrily]: Well, shit, you just don't understand.

Actually, I do understand. When you work as hard as so many teachers do, having a brilliant child in class makes you feel good. Teachers, me included, often suffer the delusion that much of a child's success is because of the teacher. That would be nice if it were true, but it isn't. A teacher can help guide a brilliant child, and certainly expose him to new ideas and experiences, but you cannot teach intelligence. Bright children make teachers feel that they're doing a fine job in the classroom, and it's understandable why we cherish that feeling, because so often we feel as if we're failing. But we have to remind ourselves that we must always try to do what's in the best interest of the student, and if that means sending him to another classroom where he has better opportunities to fly high, let him go.

My experience working with youngsters has taught me many things. It's common to have gifted students do fifty multiplication problems while other students do twenty-five, but piling on busywork is not the way to help gifted children develop their abilities. The key is to keep giving the gifted ones twenty-five problems—the twenty-five *right* ones; these children need to be challenged and worked hard, but wasting their time is no answer. If other children in class need extra practice with a math skill, why make children who have mastered the skill wait? We don't want to leave children behind, but we don't want to slow down those ready to move ahead. To complicate things further, GATE students are often used to tutor their peers who need help. There is merit to this, as it helps bright youngsters develop compassion for others. However, teachers must be careful in finding a balance here: it's nice for Johnny to take some time to help someone in need, but Johnny has needs, too. That's why it's best for Johnny to have the same hour of math but with more difficult problems, the same time for reading but with more difficult literature, and the same time for language arts but with more advanced vocabulary to study. GATE children form their own branch of special education, and just as children with learning disabilities need individualized lesson plans, GATE children need them, too.

Exposure is crucial. Gifted students need opportunities in every subject to give them the chance to develop a love of some activity in which they can then thrive. It is becoming common these days to visit classrooms in which art, music, science, history, geography, and physical education are barely taught, because the teachers are under pressure to prepare and assess their students in reading and arithmetic. At the Jungle, the school district has ordered its teachers to spend a minimum of three and a half hours per day teaching these two subjects. The entire school day is only seven hours long, and with recess and lunch taking one and a quarter hours, that leaves teachers only two and a quarter hours to teach all the other subjects we're supposed to cover. More often than not, these subjects have disappeared in elementary schools. Students, regular as well as GATE, will never discover they have a passion for mapmaking, painting, singing, biology, writing, or retracing the steps of Chief Crazy Horse. How can these children develop such interests if they don't know these things exist? I've solved the problem by lengthening my school day to cover each of these forgotten subjects. It's not rocket science. A child will more likely find something she likes to eat if there are more items on the menu.

Of these subjects, I've found music and drama to be crucial in reaching gifted students. The arts bridge the gap when kids of vastly different abilities are in the same room. With drama, a good teacher can find the right role providing the proper challenge for each individual. Recently, my fifth-graders performed an unabridged production of *King Lear*. A brilliant young girl played Goneril. It was challenging but possible for her to learn the part. Another child with less advanced language skills played a smaller role, but the experience of learning lines and being in the production was equally rewarding for her. In this way, each child can face a challenge and be part of a happy and successful fellowship of learning. If offered music, children of different abilities can be singers, dancers, and musicians. There is something for everyone.

Visitors are surprised to see that children in my class receive little homework. Because of our extended day, I don't pile it on when they go home. They work less than one hour per night. When youngsters can perform Shakespeare and solve algebra problems, it's easy to forget they're still children. Good teachers make sure the kids have time to play baseball, listen to their favorite pop star, and just look at the clouds and relax. In addition, passionate students often create homework for themselves. Students who have become fascinated with history will go home and research things that interest them. Students with a love of music practice their instruments constantly. Good readers always have homework. An exciting day of class leads to children pursuing things at home for all the right reasons.

At home, parents play a crucial role in promoting a gifted child's happiness. Caring parents often allow their excitement and pride at their child's accomplishments to interfere with his or her well-being. Practically all the gifted students I've come across have the same complaint about their parents: they can't stand having their parents compete with other parents by boasting about the abilities and accomplishments of their kids. Children often spend evenings overhearing their mom or dad on the phone telling other parents about the latest test scores or IQ results. One of two things happens when parents do this. The children grow to resent their parents' boasting and become surly. Pride becomes pressure—if they've boasted about their daughter's last test, what will happen if she doesn't do so well next time? On the other hand, some children begin to believe the hype and become arrogant and obnoxious. Either way, the message to parents is clear. It can be a blessing to have a gifted child, but treat your son or daughter as an individual. There's pressure on the child already, and comparisons with peers will lead to resentment, unhappiness, and, ironically enough, underachievement. Anxious parents should know that too much pressure will defeat the very result they're after: a highly successful son or daughter. Balance is the key for all children, and it's particularly important when eight-year-olds are being pressured to get in to Princeton.

If you have a gifted child at home, make sure he understands that being bright doesn't make him better. Outstanding ability doesn't mean your child is going to be happier, more successful, have better relationships, or even get in to Harvard. Having ability simply means that the child may have some tools that can be used more quickly, more efficiently, or more brilliantly than the ways other people use *their* tools. In many schools, where being gifted is worn like a badge of honor, arrogance soon follows and the children become full of themselves. Gifted programs need to make sure that humility is valued.

To quote the exceptional teacher Marva Collins, "I will is more important than IQ." It is wonderful to have a terrific mind, but it's been my experience that having outstanding intelligence is a very small part of the total package that leads to success and happiness. Discipline, hard work, perseverance, and generosity of spirit are, in the final analysis, far more important.

I am fortunate in having learned exactly what I want gifted children to attain. I don't have this knowledge through any particular insight or brilliance, but because I was lucky enough to meet the poster child for gifted children years ago. Her name was Joann, the very same girl whom I had insulted her first day of class when she brought me breakfast. She and her parents taught me what gifted children could be like if guided correctly.

Joann's class was a combination of fifth- and sixth-graders. I hadn't yet discovered how to teach music well to children, but I was making an effort to learn. One Christmas the kids and I were sitting around trying to work out the harmonies to a beautiful song we were going to sing for an assembly. The sixth-graders and I had a cheap little keyboard, and we were attempting to plunk out the notes that would make the harmony sections sound better. I have very little musical talent, and it really was a case of the blind leading the blind. We tried everything for about half an hour. Then Joann's quiet little voice came from the back of the room: "Try playing an F sharp, G, and A on that passage."

We tried it and it was perfect. Every head in the room turned in astonishment.

"How did you know that?" I asked in wonder.

"I have perfect pitch," she responded without a trace of pride.

I had her come to the front of the room and asked her if she played the piano. She said she did. We didn't have the sheet music to our song but had been listening to a CD. She sat down with no music in front of her and played the song exactly the way it sounded on the professional recording. The class was dazed. Kids had known her for five years and no one knew that she played. I asked her why she hadn't said anything.

"Well," she began, "I'm only a fifth-grader here, and I didn't want to take away any chance for a sixth-grader to play on the song." She meant it, too.

Later, she invited me to her house that weekend to work with me on more music for the assembly. When I walked into her bedroom I thought I had stumbled into a gold store. I had never seen more trophies and medals in my life—there were at least five hundred. I was stunned. "And these are all for music?"

"No," she corrected me, "about half are for swimming." It seems Joann forgot to mention that she was one of the top child swimmers in California. Her father asked me if I wanted to attend one of her meets, and I went the following weekend. I saw Joann swim two races. In the first, she won easily. In the second, she came in a distant second behind a young lady who would one day make the United States Olympic Team. The most interesting part of the experience was the end of both races. Both times, Joann's father was at the finish line to meet her. Both times, he helped her out of the pool, put a towel over her, and said quietly, "Good job, Jo-Jo." There was no difference in his voice responding to her victory and her loss. There was no pressure on this girl to win anything. There was only pressure to do her best, and her father's kind nature told me mountains about where Joann had learned humility, sportsmanship, and compassion.

It was one of my favorite years as a teacher. The class was

filled with delightful children, and we had a ball inside the classroom and on the road. I learned a lot from these kids, but the most important lesson came a year later. There had been one special boy in the class named Jonathan. He had a history of trouble in school. He seemed to be filled with anger but was actually quite sensitive and had a good heart. Barbara and I loved him dearly. As with many children I've taught, his home environment was not conducive to producing a happy and healthy child. I heard many rumors about the family problems Jonathan was having, but he refused to let anyone into the sadness deep within him. Jonathan came from a family where many of his relatives were in all sorts of trouble with the law, people leading him to bad places.

As a result, he often appeared to be on the outside looking in. The kids played with him in school but rarely invited him over to their homes. Jonathan went on our class trip that year, learning about the Indian Wars and following Crazy Horse's trail through the Black Hills, but when the year was over he went to a different school and separated from his old classmates. I knew I would never see him again.

As any elementary teacher knows, children love to plan surprise parties for practically any occasion. It's often for their teacher's birthday (although I think the prospect of eating candy and goodies is the prime motivation for these events). The teacher knows the kids are planning the surprise but allows them to believe they've pulled off their plan and is "stunned" when he enters the room, the lights come on, and the shouting begins. In all my years in the classroom, these children were the only ones to pull off a real surprise party—eighteen months after they had graduated from elementary school.

Joann's parents invited me over to a Christmas lunch, and

since I had gone to their home many times before, I never suspected anything. Joann asked me if I wanted to see the new piano in the garage, her rehearsal room.

When I opened the garage door, my class from the previous year was all there to perform a concert they had rehearsed for me. It was great to see them all together again. I had been in touch with most of them, and many were studying with me on Saturday mornings, but to see them all as one was delightful.

As they sang, I realized something extraordinary. Jonathan was in the middle of the mob singing, too. Over the last year, I had heard many sad rumors about this little boy. I had heard he was in trouble with both school and the law. The kids worried about him and a few tried to visit him, but he really didn't want to be seen by his old mates. I think he may have just been embarrassed, feeling he had let them down.

But there he was on this day, happy and singing. And I knew he wasn't there for me or for anything I had done for him in the class. He was there because Joann had invited him; no one else could have gotten him to accept an invitation to such a gathering, where he would have to face peers who were in much better situations than he was. She invited him because she *wanted* him to come. I learned that in Joann's world, everyone is welcome at the party, and I came to understand why she was the gold standard for my work with gifted youngsters. Joann was more than a gifted student—she was a gifted human being.

CHAPTER 12

Get Back in Line

B ut first, a word from my union . . .
I belong to United Teachers of Los Angeles and
have always believed in unions. I have never crossed
a picket line in my life, and I never will. My union staged a
strike in 1989 when I was a young teacher, and I learned
many things.

I learned above all that no matter how hard or well my
union fights for good teachers, we will never be paid what
we're worth.

I am grateful for the work UTLA has done for teachers.
We have wonderful health benefits. They fight hard to get us
higher salaries, and we all appreciate it. However, it seems
to me that the union must make one particular concession
to management: teachers must be evaluated and held accountable for their actions. How will good teachers ever be

rewarded if bad ones aren't penalized? I've met many terrific teachers who work incredibly hard and are dedicated union members. They are frustrated that terrible teachers (and there are lots of them) make us all look bad. Yet many excellent teachers are afraid to argue with the union because they don't want to sound as if we're no longer united.

We are united and will always stand behind the union. But let's face it: the schools are in terrible shape, and we are all conspirators. Parents, teachers, unions, management, politicians, businesses, and the general public share the blame in our failure to help children rise above mediocrity.

Since gaining a small amount of national recognition, I've been fortunate to meet, discuss, and share meals with many union and management officials. I've met powerful politicians who are often intelligent, articulate, and interesting. Yet in all of these meetings, there is one common defect: no one discusses the children. Many important issues are brought to the table, from politics to taxes to finances, but I have never heard anyone really talk about why Johnny can't read and calculate. Isn't that why all of us are supposed to be here in the first place?

In the end, I learned for myself the lesson a wise friend gave me the first day I walked on the picket line. She had grown up in Flint, Michigan, so unions were in her blood. "Rafe, unions are a necessary evil," she told me, "so tolerate the bullshit from both sides and never lose your focus on the kids. They are the only issue."

To all my readers who are parents or just concerned citizens, I implore you to be vigilant when it comes to the public schools. There are constant battles behind the scenes at which your presence could be beneficial.

Perhaps I have an unusual view of the world of education, but each and every day I walk into my classroom, I remind myself of something important: I remember whom I work for. It's not my principal, who is a good guy with many positive qualities. It's not any of his assistants, some of whom I like and some of whom never met Will Rogers. It is certainly not the children, although some teachers forget this and actually believe the children should have an equal voice in the daily running of a classroom.

I work for the parents and the taxpayers. They are the people who pay me and they are the people I serve. It's my job to provide them with the best service I possibly can. This is not always easy or convenient. I simply believe that anyone who becomes a teacher must accept that there are certain parts of the job not described in the contract. As a teacher, I accept the fact that not all the children will be easy to teach. I know that I will often be called on to stay after school to help a child in need. I know that large amounts of my personal time will be spent shopping for my class and planning my lessons. My wife, Barbara, a nurse for fifteen years, taught me that her shift at the hospital did not end when the clock struck a certain hour; it ended when her patients were well cared for, comfortable, and in the hands of the next shift. If that meant staying an extra hour on certain days because a patient needed a hand held or a back rubbed, Barbara was there. It was the job. The same is true for other service professions, and teaching is no different.

As a member of my union, I am ashamed to write that we forget this fact all the time. I'm happy that my union fights for me—we working people need the strength of a union to protect us from those who wouldn't otherwise give us a fair deal. I'll never leave my union, but I disagree with it constantly. In its admirable attempt to protect teachers from management that can be unfair, selfish, and just downright stupid, my union often forgets that in the teaching profession, the children are supposed to come first. The result is that the union often promotes policies that hurt good teachers and, ultimately, the children.

In an elementary school, the single most important factor in determining the progress of your child is: Who will be the teacher for the year? Your child will be spending thousands of hours with this person. We all know that the teacher creates the weather in a classroom. Will it be a happy place? Will your child be challenged without being frustrated? Will your child have a voice? Will your child learn new and exciting things? We have all been in classrooms and know that it's the teacher who holds the answers to these crucial questions.

As a parent, one of the best things you can do for your elementary-aged children should happen a few months before their next school year. This is the time when schools begin to pencil in which teacher will teach which grades. Most parents know nothing about this process. When this selection occurs, the current school year is well under way and the parents have been to Open House, have seen report cards, and have had a parent conference. Most parents assume that they've done their duty until they turn up the following year to meet the new teachers and check on their child's progress. Yet one of the most important things parents can do is to be part of the process of teacher selection for the next school year. I've seen schools where the local PTA is actually part of the hiring process, and this is as it should be.

But this isn't what happens at the Jungle and many other schools, and parents need to know what is going down.

My friend David Bryan, the charismatic and dynamic principal of New Roads School in Santa Monica, California, once told me that part of being a good principal is to have a little bit of the fascist in you. He was joking, of course, but his point was well taken. In the best circumstances at a school, a powerful but caring principal will decide which teacher will teach which class. He will consider teacher requests and personal situations, but in the end, he will ask himself which teacher is right for a particular situation and a particular group of children. When a manager of a baseball team fills out the lineup card, he chooses the best players for each spot; it's his job to put his team in the optimal position for winning the game.

Most principals are decent people. If they could have things their way, they'd examine a list of all the classes that will be taught the upcoming year, look at their roster of teachers, and create the best matches. In doing so, they would try their best to make sure that a fair system would be in place to settle things if two teachers wanted to teach the same class. Of course, the bottom line should be which teacher would do a better job, but that's not the way it usually works. Decisions can be based on connections rather than on what's best for the children, and as a result, the union's solutions can be disastrous for the kids.

Here is a look at what happens at the Jungle, and ours is not a unique situation. We have 125 teachers in the school for grades kindergarten through five. There are three different tracks for teachers to choose from, and each track has different vacation times during the year. Because teachers have their own children and lives, it's perfectly reasonable that they want to teach on a schedule that suits their family situation. They want their vacations to coincide with those of their spouses and children. The union contract states that these 125 teachers must be assigned priority numbers that determine the order in which their grades and classes are chosen. The principal is basically kept out of the decision-making loop: the teacher assigned number one gets first choice to sign up on what we call the matrix.

The amazing thing is how the priority numbers are decided. Even though the seniority system is flawed, one could argue that someone teaching thirty years should get first choice, even though this might not benefit the children, since a given class might do better with someone down the list. Yet seniority is not what prevails. Priority numbers are assigned not by ability or experience alone but also by how many district classes one has taken and whether one is bilingual. As a result, there are *terrible* teachers seeded far above the outstanding ones. Miss Excellence, one of the finest teachers I have ever known, has been teaching for thirty-five years. She is a mentor teacher and her young protégés worship her and learn excellence from her. Children in her class regularly cite her as the best teacher they've ever had, even years later when they return for a visit. However, Miss Excellence's priority number at the Jungle is 103. You're not going to believe this, but some priority numbers are given to teachers *we haven't even hired yet*! That's right, folks; because of our union contract, there have to be a certain number of teachers on each track who are new, or who are bilingual, or who are rated by factors that are completely irrelevant when measuring good teaching. Teachers with less than one year of experience, who cannot even get their classes to pay attention, are given priority over teachers who can change lives and have been doing so for many years. Please figure this out, because I can't.

This absurd situation causes problems all the time. One year after weeks of infighting, politicking, and begging, our matrix was almost complete. Teachers had submitted requests for which track and which grade they would prefer to teach. The administration met with practically everyone on an individual basis. Management and union representatives were there.

Over one hundred classrooms had to be taught, and positions had been filled and penciled in. Most of the teachers were satisfied—the administration had worked hard to give them what they desired, knowing that when teachers are happy they're going to do a better job, and everyone wins.

But inevitably, not everyone gets what he wants. Mr. Me-First, not known as a top teacher, was not happy. He received the grade he requested, but he wanted a different track and appealed to the union. According to the contract, he had the right to get a particular class in preference to other teachers who might be better qualified.

The contract was followed and he got the class he wanted. Because of this change, like dominoes, dozens of teachers had to change their tracks and grade assignments. His insistence on teaching a certain class led to the displacement of many teachers and forced a situation where hundreds of children were not assigned the teacher who would have been best for them. It doesn't make me want to sing "Look for the Union Label."

So parents, get involved with teacher selection in your

local schools. Be vigilant. Your child's future is at stake, and you may be the only one who will speak up for her interests.

Fighting between union and management hurts the children at every level. One sore spot for many good teachers has to do with salary increases. Currently, the only way a teacher can get a raise in salary is to attend classes after school or on weekends. Most teachers would acknowledge that these classes are a complete waste of time, but they attend them because the salary points earned can lead to better pay.

On the other hand, teachers are not rewarded for outstanding results. The union is firmly against any kind of merit pay, arguing that administrators would not fairly evaluate which teachers are worthy of extra money. And the union may very well be right. Judging from what some of my administrators have considered excellent teaching, I may be with the union on this one. In general, management considers teachers good if they never question the system. They want people who smile and "care about the children" as long as they don't raise issues or make trouble. I like to remind certain administrators that some of the best teachers *always* question things because they care so much that they want things to be better.

Mr. Clever is a friend of mine at the Jungle who once infuriated the administration and has never been forgiven. At a mathematics staff development session, the speaker announced that our goal for the year was to have every child in the school raise his math score above the median. Mr. Clever pointed out that it's mathematically impossible for everyone to be above the median—by definition, half of the school will be above and half below. For challenging authority in front of others, Mr. Clever, a very good teacher whose kids learn a lot, is held in disfavor by management. Anyone who is seen as an agitator is on the enemies list. On the other hand, less effective teachers who get along well with administration and never make waves might be given merit pay before Mr. Clever. Let's face it, at the Jungle, Frederick Douglass and Socrates would be given priority numbers 124 and 125.

It would be easy, when teachers stay for hours after school helping kids with homework or volunteering to supervise a club, to document the time spent and have that add up to salary points as well. With such a system, teachers would be encouraged to work longer hours and be more effective with the students. Everyone would win. But the forces of mediocrity rarely consider rewarding good teaching.

Ask any good teacher in your school (but ask quietly, away from other ears) and you'll be told the same thing. We are very happy our union is there to protect the weak. It would be helpful if it were also there to support the strong.

A look at management does not improve the picture. During the Los Angeles teachers' strike of 1989, my district provided me with one of the funniest moments of my career. It seems the district felt that replacing the striking teachers would be inconvenient but certainly possible. To lead the way, even some of the district's administrative officials planned to substitute in classrooms vacated by striking teachers. One of them, Mr. Helpless, apparently heard that I had an excellent class full of bright youngsters, and he mistakenly thought that a bright and well-organized class would be easy to teach.

The day before the strike began, I instructed the class to treat their substitute teacher with polite behavior and good manners. This worked well for the first few hours, but then it was time for math. According to what my students later told me:

Mr. Helpless: Okay, boys and girls, it's time for math. Tell me where you are in your books.

Susan: We don't have books. We're learning algebra, and our teacher can't afford to buy us algebra books. He has one book and makes copies at Kinko's every night. He left us enough work for a few weeks.

Mr. Helpless: I'm really impressed. Just think of it! Sixth-graders doing pre-algebra.

Sa Rang: Not pre-algebra. Algebra. Rafe doesn't believe in pre-algebra. He says that's a lie the district tells students who haven't been properly taught their basic arithmetic.

Mr. Helpless: I see. What are you working on?

Juan: We've been factoring polynomials.

Mr. Helpless: How do you go about your lessons?

Juan: Rafe always starts the day by asking about last night's work. We ask questions and he explains things to us until we understand.

Mr. Helpless: Oh, well, I may be a little rusty here. I was never really that good in math.

Juan: May I ask one question?

Mr. Helpless: Sure, but I'm not sure if I can help.

Juan: It's number 35. Is that a trinomial square? It looks like it, but it also seems I could pull out a GCF. What do I do?

Mr. Helpless: I really don't know. Just read the instructions and keep trying. I'm sure you'll get it.

Juan: I won't get it. I want my teacher back. He explains things very well.

Mr. Helpless: I'm sure we all want our teachers back, but for now we have to do things my way.

Juan: May I ask you a question?

Mr. Helpless: What is it?

Juan: Rafe once told me he makes $35,000 a year. I saw in the paper you make over $100,000 a year. How come you make so much more money? He's much smarter than you!

To make a long story short, Mr. Helpless became so frustrated he left the classroom. He never came back. When I returned to school after the strike, I heard the story, and I scolded Juan for being rude. But I didn't scold him much.

CHAPTER 13

Life on the Road

It's time for a horror story. I know a lot of scary ones, but this is my favorite. This tale summarizes everything that's wrong with education today and inspires me to plan my favorite activity: hitting the road with students.

Several years ago there was a controversy in Oakland. On the school holiday commemorating Dr. Martin Luther King's birthday, a shocking event took place in a movie theater. Sixty-nine high school students, all of whom happened to be African-American, were thrown out of the theater for laughing during a film. They had been watching *Schindler's List* and began giggling when the Nazis murdered one of the people in the concentration camps.

The public was outraged. They were disgusted with these students. The radio talk shows were flooded with calls. Editorial comments everywhere condemned the shameful behavior of "those punks." Oh, these terrible black kids! What's wrong with these black kids! We know they have problems, but this is just too much. How could any human being in the world laugh out loud at the murder of millions of people? It was beyond the ability of any decent human being to comprehend! There were holocaust survivors in the theater, watching the film. Had these students no shame at all?

You've got to admit, it's a horrible story. The problem was that people didn't take the time to look at the *entire* story. If they'd done so, they might have come to the same conclusion I did.

Were these students rude? Absolutely. Were they ignorant and insensitive? Of course. Did their behavior exceed any reasonable person's code of acceptable behavior? Definitely. Now here's the part the stories and talk shows left out.

The teachers were to blame.

A careful look at the entire situation revealed that the teachers did a terrible job on this outing. It was a school holiday, and four teachers were chaperons for the sixty-nine children. Here was their plan: *Schindler's List* . . . followed by ice skating! Now *there's* a well-thought-out day.

The children (yes, even in high school they're still children) had never studied World War II or the holocaust. They hadn't had any guidance on how to behave in a movie theater. There was no set of requirements to qualify for this trip in the first place.

I take large groups of students out constantly, on trips ranging from lunch and a movie to two weeks in Europe. Everywhere we go, the reaction is the same. People are amazed. The class is stopped at every museum, restaurant, or theater. Every guide or worker needs to tell me this is the politest and best-behaved class he's ever seen. Pilots and their crews have led cheers with the passengers on planes for my students. Complete strangers stop us on the street and mistakenly guess that these children come from a rich private school or church group.

How is this possible? At a time when most Americans are disgusted with the behavior of young people, why are these students so wonderful to be around? Where and how do they learn such polish and grace? Where do they acquire that sense of style that distinguishes them from other school groups? Not from me—no one has ever accused me of grace and polish. I never go to social functions and shrink when forced to be at a public gathering.

Our schools and, sad to say, some families do a very bad job with children in public places. "Kids just being kids" are often noisy and rude, spoiling a movie or museum for other people. We shouldn't accept this. We need to teach our children the proper behavior in all kinds of situations. If they're rude, let's teach them how to be polite. Just taking the kids on trips isn't enough. We as parents and teachers must do a better job if we want our children to be better human beings.

I once heard about another school that sent its fifth-graders to Washington, D.C. For their trip to the nation's capital, they spent a year getting ready and raised thousands of dollars. Yet the entire trip was only four days long, with the first and fourth days spent going and returning, leaving only two days to spend in the capital. When I spoke to one of the students to see how the trip went, she complained to me that she'd had a lousy time.

"All we did was go to the mall," the little girl told me.

"Well, that's terrific," I told her, trying to put the best face on things. "The Mall is exciting. There are the Smithsonian museums and the Washington Monument and the—"

"No, Rafe," she said. "We went to the *mall*. My teachers shopped for souvenirs and we hung out at the candy store." We can and must do better than this.

Recently, another elementary school group went to Washington. There was a story in a local school paper about the trip. Sixty children went, accompanied by twenty-two adults! Of course the adults should be commended for their commitment to the trip, but if you need twenty-two adults to supervise sixty children, the children shouldn't be going in the first place.

Nearly every year the Los Angeles Dodgers are kind enough to provide baseball tickets to several games for students at the Jungle. It's generous of them do this, but the school does a dreadful job of running the trip. Many of the kids know nothing about baseball; most don't even know who's playing. They run up and down the aisles, buying food every five minutes and screaming their heads off. The group leaves by the end of the fifth or sixth inning, and the adult leaders congratulate themselves on having taken the kids out for an evening.

I'm sorry to be so hard, but this is a waste of what could be many valuable lessons for the children. They could learn about the great game of baseball and still scream their heads off. They could eat all the food they wanted and learn to understand the sacrifice bunt at the same time. And certainly, they need to learn to finish what they start. Do we stop reading our book halfway through? Do we leave a play or movie in the middle? Leaving the game early is really teaching kids that it's okay not to finish things.

Allow me to share with you the thing that I love to do most of all: taking groups of children on the road. Hotel personnel stop us at the door and beg us to return. Restaurants throw out the bill or bring the students free desserts. Other diners in restaurants watch the group, come up to the cash registers, and pay our bills. Why does this happen?

It doesn't happen because of any brilliant teaching on my part. In fact, it happens because I've made many mistakes and stuck around long enough to learn from them. In my early attempts to travel with students, I wanted to take them places but didn't understand that I was missing opportunities for them to learn about things *that had nothing to do with the places we visited.* Instead, I mistakenly believed that having the kids walk up the steps of the Lincoln Memorial was going to be the highlight of a trip to Washington. My objectives were misguided.

I've since learned the best reason to take children on the road: *children learn and understand how to behave by being exposed to new situations and watching others.* Some children act in an inappropriate manner because such behavior is the only type they've ever seen. Children can learn how to behave appropriately at the opera if they see educated people model the manners we want them to follow. When a child accidentally touches a flame, he understands forever that fire is hot and dangerous. As a teacher of children from economically disadvantaged backgrounds, I came to understand that my students would work harder for a better life *if they saw the life they were working for.* Taking the children on trips was a chance for them to become a part of America, to feel a part of our nation rather than an unwelcome guest at the party. It's admirable to encourage students to attend college one day, but more effective to take them to universities so that they can see the possibilities. When my students had the opportunity to stay in nice hotels and observe the respectful behavior of others, they began to emulate that behavior, not because of my teaching or inspiration but through the examples they witnessed.

So parents and teachers, listen up. It's time to hit the road with a group of kids. Preparing the students for the trip is important. Once that preparation is done, the kids not only have a better time, but learning will take place in ways you could never predict. Through the opportunities these trips create, the students are allowed to discover important life lessons by themselves and, in doing so, take charge of their future lives.

But not yet. They're not ready . . . *yet.*

That is the simple secret of my method of teaching manners to young people. Politicians have a popular expression: *leave no child behind.* It sounds wonderful and generous. It's also wrong. Some children *should* be left behind. Some children are not ready to go to the movie or play . . . *yet.*

When I have a new group of fifth-grade students, I take them to the Hollywood Bowl for their first trip of the year. For those of you unfamiliar with the Bowl, it's a beautiful outdoor concert setting where classical music is played on summer nights. It's a lovely place, where people picnic and meet up with old friends and spend romantic evenings under the stars. A concert at the Bowl lasts about two hours, and we spend an additional hour before the concert having a picnic dinner together.

For my class, the evening at the Hollywood Bowl lasts two months. When the trip is announced, the first thing I do is make sure the children understand why we're going. I don't believe that Tchaikovsky is better than the rock or rap the kids are listening to at home. I do believe that it's my job as their teacher to expose the children to new and different experiences—there's no need to teach a child the latest song by the pop group of the month; the children already know that one. It's my job to teach them a new song. The kids are taught this philosophy (minds are like parachutes—they work only when they're open), and our preparation begins.

Each child is given a CD of all the music we'll be hearing that evening. Next, the child has to write a report on every composer whose music will be played at the concert. The children are then taught to play parts of the pieces we're hearing on a musical instrument, whether a keyboard, violin, or guitar. After this, students take a test on the pieces in which they must identify various passages and themes.

Then comes the final exam. We set up the class like the Hollywood Bowl. The children come in and sit down quietly. Our CD player plays the national anthem to begin the concert, and the children stand to salute the flag the same way they will if they go to the Hollywood Bowl. Finally, they listen to the entire two-hour concert silently. When the CD ends, the children clap politely.

If they're able to do all these things, they get to go to the concert. If they make noise, or become restless, or don't respond to the music, that's absolutely fine; they simply aren't ready to go *yet*. I tell these children that I still love and respect them. I explain that there are many things they can't do yet: they don't drive a car, date, or vote. And they don't do these things not because they're bad people but because they need to acquire certain skills before they're allowed to do them. When a student in my class acquires the skill necessary to spend an evening at the Hollywood Bowl, the student is invited. There's no discussion. There are no second chances. "No" is not a negotiable term. The children learn quickly that I'm kind but firm on this issue.

As a result, by the time we go to the concert, I don't have to stop the class, turn around, and say, "Okay, boys and girls, we're about to go into the concert, so be sure to be on your best behavior." They've already learned what is expected of them. They are quiet at the concert not because they believe that if they disturb others they'll get in trouble, which is the standard reason why young people follow rules—fear of the consequences if they don't. These children are quiet at the concert because they understand the music, want to hear it, and don't want to disturb the people around them. I don't even have to be there; my work was done weeks before the night of the show.

Similarly, when the class goes to a Dodgers game, they begin with a twelve-week unit on baseball. The kids learn how to play the game. They learn its history, watching the fantastic multipart documentary on baseball by Ken Burns. They also learn how to score a game and are given their own score sheets. By the time we get to the game, no one is running around worrying about food fights. We can have food fights anywhere, but watching two professional baseball teams and some of the finest athletes on the planet play the national pastime is a treat they don't want to miss. We stay until the last out. More has been learned from these experiences than merely listening to a concert or watching a game.

Here is a letter I received from a complete stranger who

observed my students eating in a restaurant in Cambria, California. I get hundreds of such letters every year, but this one is a good example of an objective person meeting students who have been taught how to behave on the road:

Dear Sir:

What a delight to have dinner with fifteen fifth-graders!

Our party of twenty-four adults from Palos Verdes had barely been seated in the Brambles Restaurant, in Cambria, when two adults brought fifteen children into this posh dining establishment, and sat them down at a long table next to ours. I know that the reaction of many in our party was that of disappointment, believing that our "adult" conversations would be interrupted by the clamor and antics of our grammar school neighbors.

Nothing could have been further from the truth!

The manners and demeanor of these fifteen students and their teacher and his wife could not have been more exemplary. These were (and are) beautiful children. At the dinner they were impeccably clean and nicely dressed. But those observations are all superficial. It was easy to see that we were dining with very happy children who were wonderfully disciplined, and whose manners were certainly no less sophisticated than those of the members of our Palos Verdes group. Various conversations around the children's table appeared both lively and interesting. I have to say "appeared" because their voices were so thoughtfully modulated that the sounds did not carry as far as our adjacent tables.

Several years ago I took forty-one children to New York City as part of a trip east. Barbara wasn't able to be with us for part of the trip, and on this particular day, I was alone with the children. We went to the Empire State Building, planning to go to the top. It was a beautiful fall day and the sun was sparkling in a stunning blue sky.

When we entered the building, we learned there was a virtual reality ride for tourists. It featured a wild trip through New York City, during which the visitors sit in a theater that seems to move, creating the illusion of enormous speed, as a movie screen shows various famous districts of New York. The kids wanted to try it and I thought it would be fun.

Tickets needed to be purchased, but the line for the movie was on a different side of the hallway. I had the forty-one children line up and asked them to wait a few minutes while I went across the hall to the ticket window to purchase their admissions. As I crossed the hall, I glanced back occasionally to make sure the children were all safe. I purchased the tickets, and as I was walking back toward my class, I watched the kind of scene that makes a teacher very happy. Ten-year-old Katherine was about to make a discovery all by herself and, in doing so, teach her classmates and teacher an important lesson.

A young man, about twenty-five, walked over to my class. It was his job to let down the restraining rope, tear the tickets, and let the crowd into the theater. As I hadn't returned, this fellow was surprised and interested in these well-mannered children waiting patiently by themselves.

Mr. N.Y.: Hey, you guys having FUN??

Kids (quietly): Uh-huh.

Mr. N.Y.: (screams): Well, you sure are QUIET!!

Janet: Well, our teacher has taught us this is a public place. We don't like to disturb anybody.

Mr. N.Y.: Waddya do for fun?

Janet: I play the violin.

Mr. N.Y.: No, I mean, waddya do for FUN??

Janet: This IS fun. I love playing the violin. When I grow up, I want to be a professional musician.

Mr. N.Y.: Lemme give you guys some advice. When you're young, raise a lotta hell. Go to the arcades. Don't listen to your teachers or parents. You're only gonna be young once, so have lotsa fun and don't worry about bein' good.

By this time, I had returned to the group. I didn't say anything; I merely passed out the tickets. We went into the theater and had a lot of fun flying all over New York City. The kids laughed and screamed and were glad we'd decided to do this before our trip to the top of the building. After we exited the theater and were standing near the elevators, I called the kids over. I was still replaying in my mind the conversation I had overheard between them and Mr. N.Y. I was a little concerned.

"Hey, you guys," I began. "Can I tell you something? I feel a little bad about this. I hope you know why we have our rules. I'm not out to spoil your fun, I'm really not. It's just that—"

"Rafe," Katherine interrupted me, "that guy takes tickets in a line for a tourist attraction. You think we're gonna listen to *him*?"

We all cracked up. "Katherine," I said proudly, "you can now leave my class. I have nothing else to teach you."

CHAPTER 14

Heroes and Villains

I'd like to give every young teacher some good news. Teaching is a very easy job. Administrators will tell you what to do. You'll be given books and told which chapters to assign the children. Veteran teachers will show you the correct way to fill out forms and have your classes line up.

And here's some more good news. If you do all these things badly, they let you keep doing it. You can go home at three o'clock every day. You get about three months off a year. Teaching is a great gig.

However, if you care about what you're doing, it's one of the toughest jobs around. If you care, and if your eyes are wide open, beware: your school is filled with bad guys. There are a few heroes around, too (no one will point them out to you—heroes are usually unrecognized). But the bad guys can be more than just mediocre teachers or administrators, incompetent individuals who do a poor job of teaching; they'll make you sad, but at least you can focus on your own students. Some bad guys will actually go out of their way to prevent you from doing your job, even when you're minding your own business.

And parents, you certainly don't want your children around such people, so be careful. Spend as much time at your school as possible. Sit in on classes. Do not be fooled by someone who appears to be a hero because he dresses well or speaks smoothly. Get to know what's really happening in the school, so that you can direct your child toward the heroes and steer her away from the villains.

Nineteen ninety-two was my Charles Dickens year. No, it wasn't because my class was reading him (we always do that). It was because for me, just as in the beginning of *A Tale of Two Cities,* it turned out to be the best of times and the worst of times.

In late 1991 a former student of mine had seen an application for the Walt Disney–sponsored American Teacher Awards. She sent it to me, practically begging me to apply for this honor. I wasn't interested and sent it back to her. This hurt her feelings. My wife advised me to consider things from the child's point of view: this student had been excited about her idea, and I had shot down her completely loving and generous thought. I apologized to her, got the form back, and carelessly filled out the questionnaire the night before it was due, figuring I could tell my student that I'd done what she wanted, forget about Disney, and get back to my students and my debts.

In the spring I took my class to Disneyland, as I did every year. There are no half measures in my class, naturally, so we went for two full days. When I got home, I picked up the mail from a few days before—I had been selected as one of the sixty finalists for the American Teacher Awards.

To make a long story short, they filmed me for a couple of days in June. Then I received another letter informing me that I had made the final cut of thirty-six teachers and would be one of three finalists representing elementary education. As luck would have it, the nationally broadcast award show was to be televised from beautiful Los Angeles. My prize was to go to an event less than three miles from my house. Whoopee!

Fortunately, I knew I wasn't going to win. The event was a four-day conference lasting from Thursday to Sunday. I didn't attend any of the activities planned for the teachers who had been flown in from all over the nation. I taught Thursday through Saturday and met the other contestants at the meals Disney hosted. All of the teachers were treated like royalty. It was a very pleasant change.

The thirty-six teachers were an interesting collection. Some of them were there because they were obviously superior teachers, the kind of people who made you proud to be in the profession. Others were there because they had overcome great personal trials and tribulations. Somehow, I wound up winning the entire thing and was crowned Outstanding Teacher of the Year. No doubt it was the swimsuit competition that clinched the top honor for me.

Seriously, though, it was thrilling to be recognized. After being interviewed and photographed until I felt like one of the Beatles, I was able to sit down for an evening with the kids to figure out how we could use my new national recognition to our advantage. We all felt that we would finally get what we always needed: a group of patrons who would support our activities with significant amounts of money. These would be the heroes who would help me overcome the odds I was up against. I started dreaming of being home evenings and weekends. I fantasized about what six or seven hours of sleep would feel like.

It wasn't going to be as easy as I thought.

I had an image in my mind of what such a hero would be like. I had already met him. Five years before the American Teacher Awards, I had taken my class to see my favorite actor on the planet, Ian McKellen, perform his extraordinary one-man show, *Acting Shakespeare*. Before the performance, our class had sent him a gift backstage. They'd written a remarkable book about Shakespeare's characters. The crowning achievement was that their verses were written in iambic pentameter and illustrated with gorgeous paintings. Our hope was that Ian would be so impressed that he might take time to say hi after the show.

I didn't understand that I was dealing with a hero. During his performance, he brought our book onstage and *read it out loud* to the audience! The crowd went wild, and when he brought my students onstage to be recognized, I was happy beyond my wildest dreams. Yet this was only the beginning. Afterward he met with my students backstage for almost two hours.

Two weeks later he invited us to San Diego and spent time with the children before his shows there. He took them around the different stages at the San Diego Old Globe Theater. He met with them in his dressing room. He made each child feel like the most important person in the world.

He writes to the children every year. When his award-winning production of *Richard III* came to Los Angeles, he brought the entire National Theatre of Britain to our classroom. When the movie was filmed a couple of years later, he had first-class buses transport over a hundred of my current and former students to MGM for a private screening. The newly knighted Sir Ian was there to spend another couple of hours with the children. When he is filming in a city and has a few spare days, he does a one-man play called *A Knight Out,* takes all the proceeds, and gives them to local charities. And whenever he's in Los Angeles, he visits our class. He even recently flew from New Zealand, where he was filming *Lord of the Rings,* to be at the children's performance of *King Lear.*

He gets it. He understands that we must support public education with actions and not just words. I mistakenly thought that with a nationally recognized classroom, my students would encounter many people with Sir Ian's values, but I was wrong. I should have remembered that Sir Ian believed in my students when I was a struggling third-year teacher. The fact that I had won some award meant nothing to him.

Backstage at the awards show, I met many of the show's sponsors. One of them was an executive with a leading national airline. With the press in hearing distance and cameras rolling, he put his arm around me and showered me with admiration. He told me he'd heard all about my travels with my class and announced that his airline would make sure that I would never again have to struggle getting my students anywhere. Trips to Washington, D.C., were to become a yearly adventure without driving me to the poorhouse. He gave me his private number and told me to call him.

I did. He was "out of the office" for the first two weeks of my calls. Finally, I reached him and we started picking dates when my class could fly to our nation's capital for a social studies trip. We picked out the cheapest time of the year to fly and the easiest days for his airline to accommodate us. I was very flexible; after all, this man was about to do me a big favor.

How big? When we had everything set, he told me that he would be able to take $5 off the price of each plane ticket. He could get me the tickets for $380 instead of the regular price of $385. What a guy!

We didn't go to Washington that year.

Some people wait for the cavalry to arrive. In our case, we wait for Hal Holbrook. This five-time Emmy Award–winning actor saw my class perform at a benefit one evening and decided to get involved. He himself had had a difficult childhood and has never forgotten his early days.

Hal is one of the busiest men I've ever known. He's always somewhere filming a movie, acting in a play, or recording his marvelous voice for a Ken Burns documentary. Yet every April, when my class performs its annual Shake-speare play, a check arrives from Hal Holbrook. He makes sure every child has books to study and supplies for school. When he's able to come and see a show, no one comes ear-lier or stays later than Hal. These children are important to him.

Of course, one of Holbrook's most famous roles is his brilliant one-man show as Mark Twain. He was completely tickled when he discovered that the ten-year-olds in my class read *The Adventures of Tom Sawyer* and *The Adventures of Huckleberry Finn* every year. Every time he performs in town, my current class is invited to see him. And after each show, Hal Holbrook takes time to talk to every child backstage—even if there are fifty children, each child gets all the time he or she needs with Hal. And when my students perform, Hal is in the audience to cheer them on. When he was speaking at the National Press Club in Washington, D.C., he gave away his time at the podium and had my students perform instead. He then went out to Planet Hollywood and had burgers with all his young admirers.

And somewhere down the road, one of these children will succeed because of the time Hal gave. Some child will make the right decision, or aim high, or not give up because a caring individual spent time with him. And Mr. Holbrook did it not because cameras were rolling but because he wanted to do it. Thank you, Hal.

I used to think people went overboard vilifying the media, but after doing countless television and radio shows, I've come to understand people's anger. The phoniness of the industry is upsetting to anyone who desires some straight talk.

My favorite media moment came when I was asked to appear on a national news show. They wanted me to debate a famous politician on educational issues. They called me on a Monday and wanted to fly me to Washington, D.C., on Friday for a television show airing Sunday. Normally, I would have declined, because I would have had to miss school, but this was a three-day weekend, so I wouldn't have to miss class. My family had planned to get away for a badly needed holiday, but we canceled our plans.

On Tuesday the producer of the show called to brief me on the topics of debate. The main point being discussed was the lack of positive parental roles in the lives of children. This is how our "pre-interview" went:

Producer: Rafe, how do you deal with so many terrible parents who lack the skills to raise their children properly?

Wouldn't you agree that poor parents are the number one problem facing teachers today?

Rafe: No, I wouldn't say that at all. Most of the parents I know are doing the very best they can.

Producer: But seriously, working in an impoverished area as you do, you must have lots of problems with the parents.

Rafe: No, I already told you I don't have problems like that. Am I not giving you the answer you want?

The next day the producer called me with a change of plans. It had been decided to have me stay in Los Angeles and debate the show's guest from a separate studio on a split screen. That was fine with me.

I was called again on Friday and told that the show had been canceled because there was going to be extensive coverage of a crisis in a foreign country. Just for the heck of it, I turned on the show during the time slot in which I was supposed to be debating the issues. Sure enough, there was the guest discussing education. The moderator announced that there was a teacher in another city ready to inform the public. The moderator asked the teacher, "Wouldn't you say that terrible parents are the worst problem teachers are facing today?"

"Yes," answered the sage teacher, "they are."

I guess I was wrong. I thought the parents I had served for many years had been interested and supportive. But they must have been terrible. After all, I saw it on television.

The funniest kinds of bad guys are the ones who think they're heroes. A local business group called my school and wanted to meet my students and me; they'd heard about the kids' musical and dramatic abilities and invited them to come to a luncheon to be honored. The kids and I drove to a five-star hotel and were escorted into a ballroom. Lunch was being served to three hundred men (there wasn't a woman in sight). The food looked and smelled great. Our host walked us past tables of food and drink and had us stand in the corner of the room, saying he'd be back in a minute.

The kids stood there for over an hour, watching the men gorge themselves while no one even offered them a glass of water. One of the kids jokingly threatened to walk over to a table and ask, in his best Oliver Twist manner, "Please sir, I want some more."

Finally, a man stood up and tapped his glass. He announced that the businessmen were proud to be supporting such a fine class. The kids then performed about twenty minutes of Shakespeare vignettes and classical music to the delight of an enthusiastic audience.

I was excited when the master of ceremonies came over and told the children they were even better than he had expected, and that we were exactly the kind of group they loved helping. We were all thrilled—I was waiting for him to take out an envelope with a check inside. I was already guessing the amount and making a shopping list for all the supplies our classroom needed.

I was wrong. He didn't reach into his pocket. He took out a bag and gave each child a pen.

"Gosh, thanks," said the children. "We really don't know what to say."

I did. "Goodbye."

Yes, I know there are many organizations and companies

that try to help our schools, so please save your ink and stamps telling me about them. But for every one of those companies, there are others that seem completely clueless about what it means to help public education. A good example of this was a local Los Angeles bank that offered its help to my class.

There is a wonderful lady with the Los Angeles Unified School District whose job it is to link up businesses and corporations that want to sponsor public school programs. She had seen many of our Shakespeare productions. We had lunch, and her idea—a marvelous one—was to perform a night of the play just for potential sponsors. I could give a talk before the performance and hand out a booklet detailing our class projects and expenses; this way, companies could pick and choose where they wanted to put their money.

The executives from the bank were fascinated to learn of our need for new books, science equipment, sports equipment, and musical instruments. Then they sat back and were dazzled by the Shakespeareans. At intermission, these businessmen shook their heads in wonder. They had never seen anything like it. Some couldn't get over the harmonies in the children's singing, their musicianship, and their ability to handle Shakespearean drama to the point where the audience forgets it's watching ten-year-olds.

After the play, the guests told me it was one of the greatest experiences of their lives, and they would be in touch soon. True to their word, within a week a large package arrived. The package had been arranged for by one of the potential sponsors. The kids and I opened it eagerly.

It was a picnic basket for two.

There was no note inside. The basket had a couple of

plastic plates and knives. I called up the woman who had arranged the event and told her I didn't understand the meaning of the basket. The woman told me the guests were so impressed that they wanted to show their appreciation "for all that you do, Rafe."

At the end of the month, when our class held its traditional auction, I sold the picnic basket to one of my students as the class laughed hysterically. I asked him if he was going on a picnic. "No," he said, "I have another plan for it."

A few weeks later I visited his house and saw the basket again. He was using it as his laundry hamper. I'm sure the generous sponsors of our class will be glad their thoughtful gift is being put to such good use.

Of course, when it comes to the support of teachers, let's not forget the insanity that takes place at the school site itself. When it comes to heroes and villains, there are plenty of both on any campus.

And before I cite some examples, an important point needs to be made. Like any veteran teacher I've met some ignorant, malicious, and downright stupid people right on the campus of a school where we're supposed to be teaching children to be wise, kind, and intelligent.

I'm not telling stories to get even with anyone, though. This is not a revenge book. Being an incredibly lucky teacher, I have no need of revenge. But I've seen teachers, just as good as but less fortunate than myself, be defeated and disillusioned by the bad guys of a school system. Therefore, I offer a few stories to help any young teacher out there prepare for the coming storm. Because if you care about your profession, if you dare to be different in any way, and if you have the courage to aim for real excellence, these negative forces will eventually marshal themselves against you as surely as Socrates asked good questions.

So, in my best Rod Serling imitation: submitted for your approval . . .

Since I teach at a year-round school, classes meet during nontraditional times of the year. Instead of from September to June, all classes at the Jungle meet for eight weeks and then have four weeks off. It's a terrible system, but this way the buildings are always occupied by 67 percent of the student body, and more kids can be serviced, if you call education at the Jungle a service.

Anyway, it was February and my class was "off track," meaning we were on vacation. The kids came to school anyway, as they always do, and we worked anywhere we could find on the campus. We'd even sit on the asphalt if lunch benches were occupied, doing extra math and reading literature.

We had come in this day because a citywide math competition was fast approaching, and my class was going to represent our school. The library was open that morning, and no one was inside, so we entered, sat down at the tables, and began our problem-solving work for the day. Suddenly, a teacher came into the library:

Miss Cruise Director: Oh, I didn't expect anyone to be here. Are you on the schedule?

Rafe: No, we're not. I'm sorry, we're off track and I didn't know your class would be using the library. Give us a minute and we'll get out of the way.

Miss Cruise Director: My class isn't using the library.

Rafe: Oh, sorry. Did you want to see me about something?

Miss Cruise Director: No, but you'll have to get out.

Rafe: I don't understand. Why do we have to leave?

Miss Cruise Director: Because we have to decorate.

Rafe: Decorate?

Miss Cruise Director: For the bridal shower.

Rafe: Excuse me?

Miss Cruise Director: For the bridal shower. One of the teaching assistants is having a bridal shower and we want the library to look nice.

Rafe: You're asking the team who will represent our school in a math competition to vacate the library so you can decorate for a bridal shower?

Miss Cruise Director: You know, Rafe, you really don't understand things. Staff morale is very important.

Rafe: More important than math?

Miss Cruise Director: What's the use talking with you? You really need to learn how to get along with people. Could you please leave, and take those kids with you?

We left, of course, and finished training outside in the rain on some benches. I stopped the session early and sent the kids home. I needed to work on getting along with people.

My team took second place at the county math championships. We were beaten by one point. I heard the shower was lovely.

It's Dr. King Day at the Jungle. We make a big deal out of honoring the man, as well America should. Class after class performs songs and skits honoring him. The children celebrate what a great American he was, and how all of them have to carry on the Dream.

As the kids do a terrific job, I sadly ponder just how far away that Dream still is. Many of the teachers have worked hard to make the day special, and yet I can't help wincing at some of the hypocrisy. Two of the teachers at the assembly approached me earlier in the year. Their daughters were about to attend high school, and they asked if I knew of any schools where there weren't any black students because "they make trouble."

We shall overcome.

Certainly most parents and school officials believe that the building of character is crucial to a successful program, but it's hard to build it in the kids when there is too little of it at the top of the pyramid.

One day something amusing happened in my class. I was giving a simple geography test in which the kids had to label a map of the United States. On this day, our elementary school was in session, but the local middle schools had a pupil-free day. This means that the students had the day off so their teachers could have meetings. Some of my former students came back to my class to visit.

During the test, one of my students was cheating. It was actually funny, because he was so bad at it. Michael kept looking at the kid's paper next to him and copying all the answers. My former students who were visiting noticed, too—you would have had to be blind not to have seen the mistake this child was making.

And before you show him any sympathy, Michael was a perfectly bright student. He was just lazy and rarely studied for exams. This day he was paying a price for his lack of effort.

After the test, my class had a meeting. I announced that there had been some cheating during the exam, and that the student guilty of the offense needed to admit his mistake in order to redeem himself. Michael raised his hand and admitted he had cheated.

"Good," I complimented him. I told him (and I meant it) that I was proud of him for admitting the wrong he had done. That was the first step toward redemption. I told him to write a letter to his parents, telling them what he had done. He would be able to take the test again tomorrow, but I wanted his parents to know about the problem. Michael thanked me for being fair with him and for giving him a second chance.

The following day I was called into the office. I was told Michael was being removed from my class and transferred into another. His parents had met with an administrator without my knowledge before school that morning and insisted that Michael would never cheat. Michael also told this administrator that he had never cheated. The administrator told me not to worry.

This is the reason teachers often throw up their hands and give up trying to instill values in their students. We are often the last line of defense in trying to teach a child right from wrong. Far too often when we try to take a stand, even in an obvious case like this, administrators don't give us the support we need.

I'm not oblivious of the difficulties of running a large school. Angry parents often come into offices complaining of a situation an administrator knows nothing about. The administrator is trying to keep everyone happy—a sort of "peace-at-all-costs" policy. Let's move Michael, calm the parents down, inform the teacher, and get on with the day.

But Michael has still cheated and has not had to face any consequences. It's moments like these when teachers become angry and eventually disheartened. We may have temporarily bought some peace with Michael and his parents, but we haven't really helped Michael at all. We will never raise children of character without the courage to make unpopular decisions.

Perhaps you are thinking that these horror stories are merely isolated incidents, and not representative of what happens in other schools. If you think that, think again. David Levin, one of our nation's most brilliant educators, had an interesting experience early in his teaching career in Houston. He questioned the system. He challenged mediocre teachers to care enough to get the job done, even if it was difficult.

Dave didn't just talk the talk; he walked the walk. He worked harder than the other teachers. With his Yale background, he was better educated than many of the other teachers. His kids loved and admired him. Soon they had some of the highest test scores in his school, his district, and eventually the state of Texas.

They should have given him a medal. Instead, Dave's fellow teachers found a different way to honor him. They slashed his tires.

Even the best days can leave a bad taste in your mouth. A couple of years ago I received a phone call with some incredible news. I was asked to speak in London at a Shakespeare conference, and my students were invited to give a performance *onstage* at the newly built Globe Theatre. Needless to say, the kids were on the ceiling.

After calming down, my fifth-graders talked it over. They came to see me after lunch and told me they shouldn't be going, that my former students who worked with me on Saturdays deserved the honor. After all, they had "put us on the map," so to speak. They felt that they themselves could travel to Europe eventually, but that the older students should go first. I was very proud of them, and true to their wishes, it was the former students who would go to London.

As the school day was almost ending, we had a surprise guest. One of my supervisors, an administrator who rarely visited, came by the room. I thought she was either lost or perhaps had come by to congratulate the kids on this tremendous opportunity.

Miss Ledger: Did I hear correctly that your class has been invited to perform Shakespeare at the Globe Theatre in London?

Rafe (beaming): Amazing, isn't it? How great for the kids.

Miss Ledger: When are you going?

Rafe: We'll be gone the second week of August.

Miss Ledger: Please let me know the dates as soon as possible. I need to know, so I can dock your pay.

Rafe: Dock my pay?

Miss Ledger: Well, you won't be here, you're not sick, so we can't pay you.

Rafe: Let me get this straight. I have worked here all these years. I work ninety minutes before school and two hours after school for no extra pay. I work every day of vacation for no pay. I work Saturday for no pay. And now, after sixteen years, you're going to dock me for taking our students to London?

Miss Ledger: Well, it would look really bad if we paid you. What if we were audited?

Rafe: I can see your point. After all, now that the Los Angeles Times *has reported that our school district just lost $200 million by building a new high school on a toxic waste dump, we wouldn't want to look bad.*

Miss Ledger: Exactly.

Later that day there was a staff meeting. Our principal told what he thought was a hilarious story. He had been trying to organize a watermelon-eating contest for lunchtime at the school. Someone had been sent in a pickup truck to buy a large number of huge watermelons, and after the truck was loaded, it tipped over.

Six, count them, six administrators had to leave the Jungle and spend four hours tracking down the lost watermelons and loading them into separate cars. That's a total of at least twenty-four hours of pay for people who made double and triple my salary. They were all laughing so hard as the story was told that they didn't notice that many of the good teachers at the school weren't laughing. They were saddened by people who worried more about watermelons than reading and docked the pay of a teacher while they made money for organizing summer-camp antics.

Incidentally, the students and I had a fantastic trip to London and helped many teachers begin teaching Shakespeare in their own classrooms. And yes, my pay was docked.

That same week, another teacher took time off to attend a friend's wedding. She was a very nice teacher and was very popular with the administration. She was paid for her time away from school.

Don't let it get you down. Just know it's there. Find the heroes in your school and draw energy and inspiration from them. At the Jungle I know a teacher who has been at it for thirty-five years and quietly goes about helping children become terrific readers. There is Rhonda, an ordained minister, whose room radiates such warmth and humanity that the children in her class are trained to be fine human beings forever. And there is Robert, a conservative man whose rigid discipline and high expectations have improved the quality of children's lives for over twenty years.

And for anyone who says there are no more heroes, you

might want to consider Matt. Matt was in my class almost twenty years ago when I taught at Camelot. He was a delightful and talented little boy. When I went to the Jungle, I never thought I would see him again. Why would I? He was awfully busy—he wound up going to Yale Law School.

Matt needed a third-year law school project, and he thought of a good one. He did the legal work to incorporate my classroom and make it permissible for me to raise funds for the children. He also arranged for them to meet a Supreme Court justice. Despite an eighty-hour workweek, he constantly brings new patrons to the class who want to help deserving children. And Matt even takes me to Laker games occasionally when he worries that I'm working too hard.

So there is hope. And there are heroes. We teachers help create them.

I'm Still Standing

It was one of those days. Every so often (not too often, but enough to remember), I experience a day of real doubt. Perhaps I was just tired.

The night before, I had received a depressing phone call. A beautiful but troubled little girl I had once known was in serious difficulties. Despite being a gifted musician and getting a scholarship to a fine music academy, she had run away from an abusive family situation. The rumor was she was now living with a man. She was fourteen.

I didn't sleep well. I was tired before the workday had even begun.

I didn't have a car, and I got caught in a surprise rain and had to walk the last two miles without an umbrella. I was cold and soaking wet when I arrived in class.

It didn't get any better. I found a memo in my box that day. Our staff had held a meeting the week before, and the teachers were given a list of ten or fifteen "extra" expenses to prioritize. The results had been tabulated. The staff had voted that having a Xerox machine was the second most important expense at our school. Our school orchestra and chorus were at the bottom of the list. Only the school nurse was rated as more important than the copy machine. Making copies was deemed more important than our orchestra, our chorus, our school psychologist, and new textbooks.

At lunch I was visited by a representative from the Multicultural Committee. The song my class had planned to perform for next week's Multicultural Day had been rejected. Our class rock-and-roll band had prepared a tight rendition of Randy Newman's brilliant "I Love L.A." I was informed that individual classes could not do performances; all fifth-grade children would dance a Swedish polka instead. The committee member who gave me this news wore a button that read "Celebrate Diversity."

My class was struggling. It was still fairly early in the year, and we had been rehearsing a very difficult play, Shakespeare's *The Winter's Tale*. Three gifted ten-year-olds were diligently attempting to play the entire Vivaldi *Four Seasons*, but progress was slow. The parts were coming along, but not as well or as quickly as I'd hoped.

After eleven hours of work, my class left quickly to go home. Many of the kids forgot to clean up their areas, and I was left with the prospect of at least ninety minutes of cleaning before a five-mile walk home.

At moments like this I wonder if it's worth it.

But there were two children who stayed behind. One of

them was Danny, the most brilliant boy in the class. Danny was the best-looking boy, the best student, the most talented musician, and the lead actor of our play. He did have a fault: he was so talented that occasionally his pursuit of excellence came off as slightly arrogant and temperamental. There were days when he became impatient and a little hard on his classmates who were trying to keep up with him. The truth is, he was a talented but sometimes difficult young man. He wasn't malicious, but he had often hurt the feelings of other people who didn't have his abilities.

The other child was Karen. She didn't stand out at first, but anyone who got to know her soon understood how special she was. She was quiet, and her soft facial features hid an inner toughness known only to those close to her. A brilliant artist, she combined her considerable talents with a work ethic that produced fine results in everything she tried.

They were the two stars of our production that year.

The girls in the class stared at Danny constantly and admired his good looks and his talent. Every girl was in love with him except one. Karen did not love Danny. And Danny, who could have chosen any other girl in the class to be his, loved Karen, the one girl who didn't love him back.

He loved her so much that in the early morning hours he would come to school before anyone else just to sit in her chair. He wrote her letters; he brought her presents; he did everything he could think of to win her. And on this evening, when I was sadly considering whether teaching was noble or just a wasted life, these two children had stayed until past six o'clock to help clean up. I was at the front of the room, going over tomorrow's lessons and setting up a science demonstration. Karen was washing the sink. Danny walked over to her, unaware that I was listening from the other side of the room.

Danny: Karen, may I ask you something?

Karen: What is it, Danny?

Danny: I don't understand you, Karen. I like you so much.

Karen: Well, I like you, too.

Danny: But not like that.

Karen: No, not like that.

Danny: All the other girls like me.

Karen: I know.

Danny: I don't understand you, Karen. All the other girls like me a lot. Why don't you like me, too? I'm so nice to you.

Karen: Because, Danny, my boyfriend has to be nice to everybody.

Danny left the room devastated. I walked slowly over to Karen, who looked me right in the eyes.

"Karen," I asked her, "how did you ever get to be so smart?"

"Because you're my teacher."

Then, as the sun set, she left the room and went home. It was almost seven and I had all the energy in the world. The walk home would be easy.

I think my next twenty years in the classroom will be even better.

ACKNOWLEDGMENTS

I could give Lou Gehrig a run for his money. My success as a teacher never would have happened without countless adults who have supported me, and children who have dared to walk the road less traveled.

There are few people who have every right to claim (and often do!) that they made me.

Sir Ian McKellen knew my class was extraordinary before I did. He was the first believer and is a constant source of strength. He is my hero.

Brandie Rose gave me her trust.

Bill Anderson wanted to help me during the hardest and loneliest of times.

Dr. Paul Cummins, brilliant and generous, allowed me to steal his patrons to create my program.

Hal Holbrook is a teacher's best friend. He makes the human race look good.

Mary Alden, Jan Miller, and Buzz McCoy are three extraordinary patrons. They are the adults behind many of the children's smiles.

Bill Graham is the best man I know. Thanks for your humor, intelligence, support, understanding, love, and most important of all, time. Thanks for making me better (as you often remind me, that's easy).

Abby Thernstrom's right balances my left. She keeps me tough.

Bonnie Solow convinced me to share with others.

Bob Gottlieb taught me *how* to share with others. Thank you for being gentle and kind, setting the tone without changing the message.

And, finally, thanks to the Hermits. You will always be the gold standard.